About this Learning Guide

Shmoop Will Make You a Better Lover*
*of Literature, History, Poetry, Life...

Our lively learning guides are written by experts and educators who want to show your brain a good time. Shmoop writers come primarily from Ph.D. programs at top universities, including Stanford, Harvard, and UC Berkeley.

Want more Shmoop? We cover literature, poetry, bestsellers, music, US history, civics, biographies (and the list keeps growing). Drop by our website to see the latest.

www.shmoop.com

Table of Contents

Introduction

In a Nutshell

Charlotte Brontë published *Jane Eyre*, a three-volume novel, in 1847 under the pseudonym Currer Bell. The novel tells the story of a young woman who, orphaned as a child, must become first a teacher and then a governess to survive. In her first post as a governess, Jane Eyre develops a romantic fondness for her employer, the craggy, rough-mannered Mr. Rochester, but she also discovers that his country estate holds mysterious and frightening secrets.

Like Charles Dickens's *David Copperfield*, *Jane Eyre* is a classic Victorian *bildungsroman*, or "novel of development." *Jane Eyre* and *David Copperfield* are also both famous for using autobiographical material from the author's life in a fictional context. In *Jane Eyre*, for example, Brontë draws on her own experiences of teaching and nursing the terminally ill, of watching her sister Maria sicken and die, and of falling in love with her supervisor while at a school in Brussels.

The most successful of the various novels by the three Brontë sisters (Charlotte, Emily, and Anne), *Jane Eyre* was an instant bestseller and has been continually in print since its first publication. Charlotte Brontë's willingness to engage, not only the titillating tropes of Gothic fiction and the difficulties facing unmarried middle-class women, but also the problems of empire and colony in 19th century England, has created a hybrid text that remains relevant and interesting for 21st century readers. Readers can focus on anything from the details of interpersonal relationships and romances to the fear and suspense of the Gothic genre or the problems of nationalism.

Viewing audiences have also embraced the story; *Jane Eyre* has been adapted for film and television more than two dozen times over the last century, from a 1910 silent version to the 2009 film currently in production, and has also been transformed into a musical, a ballet, and an opera.

Why Should I Care?

When you look at *Jane Eyre*, you might just see a long novel about a gal in an ugly gray dress whose life – a lot of the time – totally sucks. Whether she's gagging on burned porridge at her horrible boarding school or discovering that her fiancé is already married to someone else or wandering around on the moor starving to death, life is often painful for Jane.

The thing is, it's not painful to read about it. In fact, we start to get kind of obsessed with all the gory details after a while. Did Jane and Rochester's wedding really get interrupted at the altar just now? When did Rochester decide to keep his wife locked in the attic? How many mistresses did he have? Is he Adèle's dad or not? Will Jane marry her cousin or agree to bigamy? Is there a ghost at Thornfield Hall or is it a vampire? They could make a reality show out of this; it would be like *Supernanny* + *The Bachelorette* + *Ghost Hunters*.

Of course, apart from the whole thirst-for-voyeurism thing that we all have, *Jane Eyre* also about something else: The Man getting you down. Over and over, Jane's put into situations where she's too young, too poor, or too powerless to win, but she has to try anyway, and we all know about that. We've all been the kid who was completely mistreated by some random adult like Mrs. Reed or Mr. Brocklehurst just because that person has a stick up you-know-where. We've all had to accept that everyone would believe the adults just because they are adults, so they get away with it. Maybe some of us have also been the young employee who gets pressured to do something immoral by our boss. Or the girlfriend who finds out that her boyfriend's taking someone else out on Friday night. That "someone else" might not be an insane vampiric arsonist, but hey, parallels only go so far.

What we're trying to say is: half of *Jane Eyre* is pure get-the-popcorn omigosh-she-didn't spectacle, and the other half is looking pretty familiar.

Summary

Book Summary

Jane Eyre is the story of a young, orphaned girl (shockingly, she's named Jane Eyre) who lives with her aunt and cousins, the Reeds, at Gateshead Hall. Like all 19th century orphans, her situation pretty much sucks. Mrs. Reed hates Jane and allows her son John to torment the girl. Even the servants are constantly reminding Jane that she's poor and worthless. At the tender age of ten, Jane rises up against this treatment and tells them all *exactly* what she thinks of them. (We wish we could've been there to hear it!) She's punished by being locked in "the red-room," the bedroom where her uncle died, and she has a hysterical fit when she thinks his ghost is appearing. After this, nobody knows what to do with her, so they send her away to a religious boarding school for orphans – Lowood Institute.

At Lowood, which is run by the hypocritical ogre Mr. Brocklehurst, the students never have enough to eat or warm clothes. However, Jane finds a pious friend, Helen Burns, and a sympathetic teacher, Miss Temple. Under their influence, she becomes an excellent student, learning all the little bits and pieces of culture that made up a lady's education in Victorian England: French, piano-playing, singing, and drawing. Unfortunately, an epidemic of typhus breaks out at the school, and Helen dies. (We always knew she'd be a martyr.) Jane remains at Lowood as a student until she's sixteen, and then as a teacher until she's eighteen. When Miss Temple leaves the school to get married, Jane gets a case of wanderlust and arranges to leave the school and become a governess.

The governess job that Jane accepts is to tutor a little French girl, Adèle Varens, at a country house called Thornfield. Jane goes there thinking that she'll be working for a woman named Mrs. Fairfax, but Mrs. Fairfax is just the housekeeper; the owner of the house is a mysterious Mr. Rochester, and he's Adèle's guardian, although we're not sure whether she's his daughter. (Yep, this is getting exciting!) Jane likes Thornfield, although not the third floor, where a strange servant named Grace Poole works alone and Jane can hear eerie laughter coming from a locked room.

One evening when Jane's out for a walk, she meets a mysterious man when his horse slips and he falls – and, of course, this is Mr. Rochester. Jane and Rochester are immediately interested in each other. She likes the fact that he's craggy, dark, and rough-looking instead of smooth and classically handsome. She also likes his abrupt, almost rude manners, which she thinks are easier to handle than polite flattery. He likes her unusual strength and spirit and seems to find her almost unworldly; he's always comparing her to a fairy or an elf or a sprite.

Rochester quickly learns that he can rely on Jane in a crisis – one evening, Jane finds Rochester asleep in his bed with all the curtains and bedclothes on fire, and she puts out the flames and rescues him. Jane and Rochester have fascinating conversations in the evenings and everything seems to be going really well…until Rochester invites a bunch of his rich friends to stay at Thornfield, including the beautiful Blanche Ingram. Rochester lets Blanche flirt with him constantly in front of Jane to make her jealous and encourages rumors that he's engaged to Blanche. Don't worry, though – it's really only Jane he wants.

During the weeks-long house party, a man named Richard Mason shows up, and Rochester seems afraid of him. At night, Mason sneaks up to the third floor and somehow gets stabbed and bitten (ew). Rochester asks Jane to tend Richard Mason's wounds secretly while he fetches the doctor. The next morning before the guests find out what happened, Rochester sneaks Mason out of the house.

Before Jane can discover more about the mysterious situation, she gets a message that her Aunt Reed is very sick and is asking for her. Jane, forgiving Mrs. Reed for mistreating her when she was a child, goes back to take care of her dying aunt. When Jane returns to Thornfield, Blanche and her friends are gone, and Jane realizes how attached she is to Mr. Rochester. Although he lets her think for a little longer that he's going to marry Blanche, eventually Rochester stops teasing Jane and proposes to her. She blissfully accepts.

Everything seems to be going great, until we notice that there's still a third of the book left. That means something bad is about to happen.

It's the day of Jane and Rochester's wedding. It should be the happiest day of Jane's life, but during the church ceremony two men show up claiming that Rochester is already married! (Is this sounding like a *Jerry Springer* episode yet?) Rochester admits that he is married to another woman, but tries to justify his attempt to marry Jane by taking them all to see his "wife." Mrs. Rochester is Bertha Mason, the "madwoman in the attic" who tried to burn Rochester to death in his bed, stabbed and bit her own brother (Richard Mason), and who's been doing other creepy things at night. Rochester was tricked into marrying Bertha fifteen years ago in Jamaica by his father, who wanted him to marry for money and didn't tell him that insanity ran in Bertha's family. Rochester tried to live with Bertha as husband and wife, but she was too horrible, so he locked her up at Thornfield with a nursemaid, Grace Poole. Meanwhile, he traveled around Europe for ten years trying to forget Bertha and keeping various mistresses. Adèle Varens (Jane's student) is the daughter of one of these mistresses, though she may not be Rochester's daughter. Eventually he got tired of this lifestyle, came home to England, and fell in love with Jane.

After explaining all this, Rochester claims that he's not really married because his relationship with Bertha isn't a real marriage. The main problem is that he can't divorce her (because it was pretty tough to get a divorce at all in the Victorian period, and Bertha's behavior isn't grounds for a divorce, since she's mentally ill and therefore not responsible for her actions). He wants Jane to go and live with him in France, where they can pretend to be a married couple and act like husband and wife. Jane refuses to be his next mistress and runs away before she's tempted to agree.

Jane travels in a random direction away from Thornfield. Having no money, she almost starves to death before being taken in by the Rivers family, who live at Moor House near a town called Morton. The Rivers siblings – Diana, Mary, and St. John – are about Jane's age and well-educated, but somewhat poor. They take whole-heartedly to Jane, who has taken the pseudonym "Jane Elliott" so that Mr. Rochester can't find her. Jane wants to earn her keep, so St. John arranges for her to become the teacher in a village girls' school. When Jane's uncle Mr. Eyre dies and leaves his fortune to his niece, it turns out that the Rivers siblings are actually Jane's cousins, and she shares her inheritance with the other three. (Now she's *Jane Heir*, ha ha.)

St. John, who is a super-intense clergyman, wants to be more than Jane's cousin (back when that wasn't considered gross). He admires Jane's work ethic and asks her to marry him (how un-romantic), learn Hindustani, and go with him to India on a long-term missionary trip. Jane is tempted because she thinks she'd be good at it and that it would be an interesting life. Still, she refuses because she knows she doesn't love St. John. To top it off, St. John actually loves a different a girl named Rosamond Oliver, but he won't let himself admit it because he thinks she would make a bad wife for a missionary.

Jane offers to go to India with him, but just as his cousin and co-worker, not as his wife. St. John won't give up and keeps pressuring Jane to marry him. Just as she's about to give in, she supernaturally hears Mr. Rochester's voice calling her name from somewhere far away.

The next morning, Jane leaves Moor House and goes back to Thornfield to find out what's going on with Mr. Rochester. She finds out that Mr. Rochester searched for her everywhere, and, when he couldn't find her, sent everyone else away from the house and shut himself up alone. After this, Bertha set the house on fire one night and burned it to the ground. Rochester rescued all the servants and tried to save Bertha, too, but she committed suicide and he was injured. Now Rochester has lost an eye and a hand and is blind in the remaining eye.

Jane goes to Mr. Rochester and offers to take care of him as his nurse or housekeeper. What she really hopes is that he'll ask her to marry him – and he does. They have a quiet wedding, and after two years of marriage Rochester gradually gets his sight back. St. John Rivers, meanwhile, goes to India alone and works himself to death there over the course of several years.

Volume I, Chapter One

- *Jane Eyre* begins with the adult Jane looking back at her life. She jumps into the story at a moment in her childhood when she's ten years old.

- On this particular day, Jane and her cousins John, Eliza, and Georgiana aren't going to do something: they're not going to take a walk, because it's too wet. Jane is relieved; she hates walks, because it's depressing to realize that she's not as physically hardy as her cousins.
- Jane's cousins – Eliza, John, and Georgiana – are "clustered round their mama" (1.1.3), but Jane's not allowed to join them, because her aunt, Mrs. Reed, and her nursemaid, Bessie, claim that she's been naughty. Jane has no idea what she's supposed to have done.
- Jane goes into the breakfast room, climbs up into the window seat, pulls the red velvet curtains around her (apparently the Reeds are pretty rich), and reads Bewick's *History of British Birds*, which is sort of like an illustrated field guide. She likes the pictures and the descriptions of icy landscapes – maybe this penchant for arctic places is supposed to tell us something about her?
- Jane's cousin, John Reed, goes looking for her and, with the help of his sister Eliza, finds her in the window seat. We can tell that he's seriously bad news.
- Jane tells us a little bit about John Reed: he's fourteen, big, a greedy eater, pampered by his mom, doesn't really like his family, and especially hates Jane. He is, basically, a big fat bully.
- After a long pause, John smacks Jane really hard. He makes her show him which book she was reading, and then lords it over her that she's dependent on his family and tells her she can't read his books. Then he throws the book at her hard enough to knock her down, and she cuts her head on the door.
- Jane jumps up and tells John off, calling him "wicked and cruel" and "like a murderer" or "like a slave driver" or "like the Roman emperors" (1.1.33). He grabs her and they start fighting. Jane's not sure what she does, but she must hurt him somehow because she makes John holler.
- Eliza and Georgiana go and get their mother, Mrs. Reed, and the nursemaid Bessie, like the little tattletales they are.
- Jane's blamed for the fight, and Mrs. Reed orders that she be locked in "the red-room"...that doesn't sound sinister or anything, right?

Volume I, Chapter Two

- The nursemaid, Bessie, and Mrs. Reed's lady's-maid, Miss Abbot, physically drag Jane to the red-room; she's fighting them the whole way, which, she tells us, is unusual for her, but she's half-crazed.
- Jane objects to John Reed being called her "master," and Miss Abbot tells Jane that she is "less than a servant" because she doesn't even work or pay for her room and board. We think this is pretty harsh – after all, she's ten, and the Reeds are rich.
- Bessie and Abbot plunk Jane down on a stool; they threaten to tie her down, but she promises to stay in place.
- The servants spend a few minutes reminding Jane *again* that she's just a poor orphan, that she ought to be grateful to her aunt for taking her in, and so on. They even claim that

God will strike her down if she keeps having tantrums, and then they leave and lock her in.

- Jane tells us about the red-room, which is a spare bedroom furnished in, you guessed it, red – red curtains, red carpet, red tablecloth, reddish wood (mahogany) furniture – although there are a few white things in it, too. It's cold, quiet, and lonely, and...here's the creepiest bit...it's the room in which her uncle, Mr. Reed, died (of natural causes).
- Jane gets up to make sure she's locked in – yep, she is. Then she looks in the mirror, and the room looks *even weirder* in the mirror, especially because her reflection looks sort of like a ghost. Hint: this isn't the last time that Jane herself will seem almost supernatural.
- Jane thinks about how unfair her situation is – she's bullied by her cousins, her aunt hates her for no reason, and even the servants are snotty to her. She knows that she's the best behaved of the four children, but everyone dislikes her and indulges the others, and this unfairness really bothers her. Her keen ethical sense is awakening!
- Jane the child, whom we're following in the story, can't understand why she's being mistreated, but the older adult Jane, who is telling the story (see "Narrator Point of View"), can. It's not because she's poor, but because she's different than the Reeds – different in temperament. Maybe, she thinks, it's also because Jane is only Mrs. Reed's niece by marriage; she was related to Mr. Reed, but she and Mrs. Reed aren't blood relatives.
- It's starting to get dark and the wind and rain are still raging outside – Jane's beginning to freak out in this creepy red-room.
- Jane decides that if Mr. Reed were here now, he would be nicer to her than his widow and children are...but then she starts to worry that he might come back from the grave to try to comfort her, and that would be *creepy*.
- Jane tries to calm down so that Mr. Reed's ghost doesn't appear to reassure her, but then she sees a weird streak of light. Where is it coming from? It's not the moon. Is it a lantern? Maybe. Is it a ghost? EEEK! Jane screams. Well, actually, she "utter[s] a wild involuntary cry" (1.2.32), but you get the idea.
- Bessie and Abbot come running and ask what's the matter. Bessie seems sympathetic when Jane tells her that she thought she saw a ghost – she lets Jane hold her hand – but Abbot thinks that Jane is just trying to trick them into letting her out.
- Next Mrs. Reed comes to see what all the noise was. Uh-oh. She's mad that the servants didn't obey her orders to leave Jane alone and, like Abbot, she thinks that Jane's being manipulative.
- Mrs. Reed punishes Jane with another hour alone in the red-room, and as she leaves Jane faints.

Volume I, Chapter Three

- Jane wakes up, confused and disoriented. Someone is holding her gently; she's never been held gently before.
- She starts to realize where she is – in her own bed. Bessie and a gentleman are there, looking after her.
- Jane's glad to see the gentleman, because he's not one of the Reeds. She looks at him closely and realizes that she knows him. It's Mr. Lloyd, a local apothecary (sort of like a pharmacist – he can give out prescriptions and medicines, but he doesn't have a doctor's

training).
- Mr. Lloyd gives Bessie instructions about looking after Jane and says he'll come back tomorrow, then leaves. Jane feels really depressed after he leaves; he's much nicer to her than anyone else who lives at Gateshead (Mrs. Reed's home).
- Bessie offers to get Jane something to eat or drink and is generally really nice to her. Jane's pretty confused by this kindness.
- Bessie goes into another room, and Jane overhears her ask the housemaid, Sarah, to sleep in the nursery because she's scared that Jane could die.
- Sarah and Bessie come back to sleep in the nursery; Jane listens as they whisper about strange figures and visions that were seen around Jane earlier – something dressed in white, a black dog, lights, noises. They fall asleep, but Jane's wide awake in terror.
- Jane tells us that, even though she doesn't get sick after this shock, her nerves never really recover. She blames Mrs. Reed, even though she knows that maybe she shouldn't.
- When Jane gets up the next day, she sits by the fire wrapped in a shawl; the Reeds have gone out somewhere, Abbot is sewing, and Bessie's tidying up. Jane should be happy to be left alone for once, instead of bullied and tormented, but she can't stop crying silently to herself.
- Bessie brings Jane a treat – a tart, and on a beautiful china plate that Jane's always liked. She can't bring herself to eat it.
- Next Bessie asks if Jane wants a book; she asks for *Gulliver's Travels* , which she's always loved (and thinks is nonfiction). But even reading can't comfort her now; Gulliver seems lonely and beset by terrible dangers.
- As she works, Bessie starts singing a song that Jane has always liked in the past. But this time – can you guess? – yep, it just sounds sad. We're starting to wonder if Jane will ever enjoy anything again.
- Mr. Lloyd comes to see how Jane is doing. She's not sick, and he starts trying to figure out why she's so miserable.
- Bessie tells Mr. Lloyd things that make Jane sound babyish: that she's crying because she didn't get to go out in the carriage with everyone else, and that she was sick because she had a fall. Jane's pretty indignant about these charges and denies them both – and explains that the "fall" was actually when John Reed knocked her down.
- A bell rings and Bessie has to go have dinner with the other servants, so Mr. Lloyd is left alone with Jane.
- Jane tells Mr. Lloyd about the ghost, and he finds that pretty silly.
- Jane protests that she's miserable for lots of other reasons: she doesn't have any immediate family, Mrs. Reed and her son John are cruel to her, and she's made to feel that she doesn't have any right to live at Gateshead.
- Mr. Lloyd starts asking about different ways Jane could leave Gateshead. Does she have any other family? She's not sure, but she doesn't think so, and she wouldn't want to live with them if they were poor anyway. Could she go to school?
- Jane thinks about school. She's heard bad stuff about school from Bessie and John, but she doesn't really trust either of them, and she is interested in learning to paint and sing and sew and read French and stuff – the things she knows young ladies get taught in school. Plus, she'd be able to get away from the Reeds.
- Jane tells Mr. Lloyd that she does want to go to school, and he advises Mrs. Reed to send her to one.
- Jane hears Abbot tell Bessie that Mrs. Reed will send Jane to school, if only to get rid of

her. Jane also hears Abbot talk about her (Jane's) own family: her dad was a poor clergyman (like a minister), and her grandfather disinherited her mother for marrying him, and both of them (Jane's mom and dad) died while taking care of sick people during a typhus outbreak. Well, at least now she knows where she comes from.
- Bessie and Abbot agree that they would be able to feel sorry for Jane "if she were a nice, pretty child" (1.3.78) or "a beauty like Miss Georgiana" (1.3.79), but they can't really feel bad for her because she's unpleasant and ugly. We think they're *jerks*, especially for saying this in front of Jane. Hollywood movies may not show it, but you don't have to be stunningly gorgeous to suffer, you know.

Volume I, Chapter Four

- Jane is waiting patiently, convinced that Mrs. Reed will send her to school soon, even though she hasn't said so.
- Jane seems to be in more disgrace than usual: she has a smaller room, eats alone, and none of the Reed children are even speaking to her.
- John tries to say something nasty to Jane, but she hits him on the nose and he runs crying to his mom. We can hardly believe that he's fourteen.
- This time, Mrs. Reed won't listen to it, and tells him to leave Jane alone. She makes it sound like she's being snobby, saying that her children won't "associate with" Jane (1.4.3).
- Jane says that the Reed children "are not fit to associate with" her anyway (1.4.5). Mrs. Reed freaks out and attacks Jane, who asks what Mr. Reed would say if he were still alive. Her aunt seems frightened by this, but not too frightened to box Jane's ears. Bessie lectures Jane about being wicked.
- Time passes. Christmas comes and goes and Jane doesn't get any presents or any chance to participate in the festivities. Even Bessie leaves her alone, and so Jane has to sit in the dark and take care of her doll, which is the only thing she has to love. It's pretty pathetic.
- Jane-the-narrator (the older one, remember? See "Narrator Point of View") reminisces about Bessie: sometimes the nursemaid is kind to her or brings her treats, and she tells such great stories! She does have a bad temper and no real ideas of ethics or justice, but she's all Jane has at Gateshead.
- One day, things start to change. Jane paints us a picture of what's happening on this particular day: it's early in the morning; Eliza, who, we learn, loves money a *little* too much, is getting ready to go out and feed the hens she keeps so that she can sell the eggs; Georgiana is doing her hair in the mirror; Jane is tidying up as Bessie ordered.
- From the window, Jane sees a carriage, but she isn't really paying attention to it because she doesn't think it will matter to her. She starts feeding a bird some of her breakfast on the window-sill.
- Bessie comes bustling in, freaking out because Jane hasn't washed yet and is red in the face from leaning out into the cold air. She cleans Jane up and makes her presentable and sends her downstairs.
- Jane's confused and scared; she hasn't been sent to see Mrs. Reed for almost three

months. She's afraid to go into the breakfast-room, but afraid to disobey. She stands still for a long time.

- When Jane finally goes in, she sees a tall man dressed in black, who has a "grim face [...] like a carved mask" (1.4.22). Does that sound good to you? Nope, it doesn't to us either.
- The man starts asking Jane questions. She tells him her name, but when he asks if she's "a good child" (1.4.30), she doesn't know what to say – she knows Mrs. Reed will contradict her if she answers yes.
- The man assumes that this means Jane is naughty, and starts lecturing her on how wicked children go to hell. We're definitely starting to dislike him, and so is Jane.
- The man asks Jane about reading her Bible. She does, and she tells him about the parts she likes, which are mostly exciting things like Revelations and Daniel. She tells him up front that she doesn't like the Psalms because they're not very interesting, and he says that she has "a wicked heart" (1.4.56) and should pray to God to change it. He's pretty tiresome. We can only hope he's not in the book for very long.
- Mrs. Reed steps in at this point; she doesn't really care about Jane's heart. She reminds Mr. Brocklehurst (that's apparently his name) that she already told him Jane is unpleasant and a liar and needs special watching at Lowood school, which is where he's going to take her.
- Jane is really upset that Mrs. Reed accuses her of being a liar in front of Mr. Brocklehurst, who is obviously someone important at Lowood. She can tell Mrs. Reed is just making things harder for her at her new school.
- Mrs. Reed also insists that Jane be "made useful" and "kept humble" (1.4.62) at Lowood. Mr. Brocklehurst is only too happy to oblige; he loves keeping the girls at the school "quiet and plain" (1.4.63). As he describes them, though, it becomes clear that his own daughter lives in spoiled luxury – she has a silk gown. So Mr. Brocklehurst is a hypocrite in addition to being nasty.
- Mrs. Reed is happy; now that she knows Mr. Brocklehurst will keep Jane down, she's ready to send her to Lowood.
- As he leaves, Mr. Brocklehurst gives Jane a book called the *Child's Guide* , full of stories about sinful children who die unpleasantly. He tells her to read the story about Martha, who is a liar. How sweet.
- Jane stands staring at Mrs. Reed and refuses to leave the room when she's ordered to. She is *pissed*. She confronts Mrs. Reed, denying that she (Jane) tells lies, saying she hates Mrs. Reed and John, and that the book about Martha the Liar is more appropriate for Georgiana than Jane. Ouch! That's a bit too honest.
- Mrs. Reed asks what else Jane's going to say. Jane's only started. She disowns her aunt and says she'll never come to see her as an adult and that she'll tell everyone how badly Mrs. Reed treated her. Jane describes how Mrs. Reed treated her in the red-room episode, and shows Mrs. Reed her own cruelty and deceitfulness.
- After Jane tells Mrs. Reed off like this, she feels really good. In fact, she feels exultant. The truth has set her free, and all that. Well, kind of free. She's still a dependent child.
- Mrs. Reed is really disturbed – so disturbed that she gets up and leaves Jane in the room. Jane feels like she has won a battle and taken possession of the "field" (1.4.95).
- After a while, Jane stops feeling so good. She knows that this will just make her situation worse in the long run, and she wants to feel good for a better reason than "fierce speaking" (1.4.97).
- Jane does what she always does when she needs to be comforted: she starts reading a

book, but can't concentrate.
- Jane goes outside and walks in the wintry landscape, feeling terrible.
- Bessie calls Jane, but she doesn't come. Bessie has to go get her.
- Jane coaxes Bessie into a good mood, and they have a rare, pleasant afternoon together while the Reeds are out at tea.

Volume I, Chapter Five

- Jane leaves Gateshead, refusing to say anything to Mrs. Reed before she goes.
- Bessie takes Jane to the porter's lodge, and then takes a coach by herself for fifty miles to get to Lowood. The journey takes a long time, and she's afraid of being kidnapped, which is something that happened a lot in Bessie's stories.
- At the end of the coach trip, a woman (we learn later that her name is Miss Miller) meets Jane and takes her to a building. We assume this is Lowood School, but nobody has bothered to tell Jane where she is.
- Jane meets a tall, dark-haired woman who seems to be in charge (later we find out her name: Miss Temple). She's quite nice and asks Jane about her background, then has Miss Miller take her to a large hall, where about 80 other girls are studying.
- Monitors collect the girls' books, and everyone is served "supper," which is just water and some oaten cake things. Gross, right?
- Jane is sent to sleep with the other girls in a long hall. Everyone sleeps two to a bed, and Jane is sharing with Miss Miller.
- Everyone gets up before dawn to study math and listen to some Bible reading. Sounds great, doesn't it?
- Breakfast is burned porridge, which nobody is really able to eat because it's so disgusting. Apparently this isn't the first time that's happened. Jane can't eat; she's busy studying her new teachers.
- Jane notices how plainly all the girls are dressed; nobody has curled hair, and everyone is wearing ugly brown wool gowns with weird pockets on the front.
- The first lesson is geography, but Jane still can't pay attention, because Miss Temple, who is the superintendent (like the principal) comes in again and Jane is, um, very taken with her. In fact, she practically worships Miss Temple, starting from this moment.
- Miss Temple decides to give the girls bread and cheese for lunch to make up for the burned porridge. Apparently it's pretty major for the girls to actually get extra food; everybody's surprised.
- Everyone gets to go out into the garden for a bit, but because it's winter things are pretty bleak outside. Jane starts talking to a girl (we don't learn her name until Chapter Six, but it's Helen Burns) who is sitting alone reading, and the girl tells her about the school: Lowood Institution, a charity school for orphans. Mr. Brocklehurst is in charge of it all, and we know how much he likes Jane! This is going to go *really well*, we can tell.
- Everyone has another gross meal and keeps studying until five o'clock. If you're doing the math, this probably means that, with a few short breaks, school has taken more than twelve hours already. Yikes.
- Jane sees Miss Scatcherd punish Helen by making her stand alone in the middle of the

room while everyone else works. Jane would be ashamed in her place, but Helen is quiet and dignified, and Jane admires her.

- More small amounts of plain food and prayers, and it's bedtime. After one day at the school, Jane can tell this is going to be pretty lame. Lowood makes us appreciate our schools, that's for sure. At least we never had to eat burned porridge.

Volume I, Chapter Six

- Everyone gets up before dawn again and it's so cold that the water inside is frozen, so they can't wash. At least the porridge is OK this morning.
- Jane starts having to actually do lessons with everyone else, which include sewing.
- While she's sewing, Jane watches another group of girls doing English history lessons with Miss Scatcherd. Remember that teacher who always picked on you for every little thing you did, including breathe? Well, that's how Miss Scatcherd is with Helen Burns. She doesn't like the way Helen stands, or the way she holds her head, or anything, even though Helen's really smart and good at her lessons.
- Eventually Miss Scatcherd gets angry enough about whatever it is that's biting her that she whips Helen's neck with a bundle of twigs. Well, at least that doesn't happen in school anymore, even if they do make you go to assembly sometimes.
- Jane wanders around alone during the free time in the evening, but she doesn't really feel bad; after all, her home at Gateshead was crumby, too.
- Jane finds Helen and talks to her, learning her name for the first time. She can't understand why Helen isn't more upset about how Miss Scatcherd treats her; she knows she'd freak out if she had been in Helen's place.
- Helen is disgustingly good and patient and reminds Jane about turning the other cheek and all that sort of thing. We're guessing she'll die young, because nobody this perfect ever lives to be 40.
- Helen agrees with all Miss Scatcherd's criticisms of her, which Jane thinks is just stupid, since Helen is obviously great. Helen admits to daydreaming quite a bit, but we don't think that's a fault. Plus, she daydreams about important history-lesson-type stuff, like why Charles I was a bad king, not about lame things like what color to paint her nails next (not that anyone paints their nails in this book anyway).
- Helen does admit that Miss Temple treats her differently from Miss Scatcherd, but she says that's her own fault for being a better person when Miss Temple is around. Jane thinks, and we agree, that maybe Miss Temple is just a better teacher and a nicer person than Miss Scatcherd, but this hasn't occurred to Helen.
- Helen's "love your enemies" stuff starts to drive Jane crazy, and so Jane tells her about how impossible it is for her to love that harpy Mrs. Reed. After hearing the whole story, Helen's only answer is that Jane shouldn't let herself get so obsessed with being angry at Mrs. Reed. We don't know how exactly that's supposed to work, but Helen doesn't get a chance to explain, because she just got in trouble for something else.

Volume I, Chapter Seven

- Jane continues to settle in at Lowood, if you can call it settling in. Not only does she have to learn all the new school rules and the course material, she also has to cope with the fact that nobody in the school ever gets enough to eat and they're always cold because their clothes are thin and old. There's an especially gross description of chilblains (sores from exposure to the cold) on her hands and feet. We're not sure if we're more sorry for her or grossed out.
- The little girls suffer most, because the older girls steal their food and crowd them away from the fires. Our heroine, of course, usually gives some of her food away to the smaller girls who are actually starving. Awww, isn't that sweet.
- Despite all the hardships, Miss Temple encourages all the girls and motivates them to keep going. All the other teachers are too depressed to try, and we can't really blame them.
- After Jane has been at the school for three weeks, as if things weren't bad enough, that hypocrite Mr. Brocklehurst shows up to visit and inspect the school. This is going to go really well, we're sure.
- Jane hears Mr. Brocklehurst giving Miss Temple "instructions" about how to run the school. Well, that's the nice way of putting it...he's mostly just nitpicking and trying to make her be colder and crueler to the girls.
- Mr. Brocklehurst is especially upset about the two times Miss Temple served the girls an extra lunch to make up for their burned porridge. He has a long, plausible-sounding explanation of why it would be better for their *souls* and their *temperaments* if they just took the opportunity to think of their hunger as a happy Christian martyrdom. We don't know when Mr. Brocklehurst himself last missed a meal, but we're guessing it was a long, long time ago.
- The other thing that's biting Mr. Brocklehurst is the hairstyles of various girls. None of the girls at Lowood are supposed to curl their hair, so *why,* he wants to know, does Julia Severn have curls in her hair? Of course, that's because her hair curls naturally, but so what? Mr. Brocklehurst knows that, if she can't get her hair straight, then she should just cut it all off to be humbler. He says he'll send the barber tomorrow to cut her hair – and the hair of all the older girls, who have been wearing fashionable top-knots. Those *hussies.* They've been *doing their hair*. Now that's sin, right there, isn't it? We hope they repent.
- At this point, Mr. Brocklehurst's wife and daughters enter and interrupt his kind-hearted, sweet-natured, humble instructions. As befits the family of so pious a clergyman, they wear plain woolen gowns and have their hair combed flat against their heads. NOT. You didn't believe that, did you? Actually Mrs. Brocklehurst and her daughters are all dolled up in fancy gowns of expensive silk, velvet, and fur, with fashionable hats, delicately curled hair, the works. They've been upstairs, snooping around in the girls' rooms, making sure none of *them* own anything too fancy.
- Jane tells us that she's been hunkering down behind her slate, hoping really hard that the Brocklehursts will come and go without noticing her. And they would – except she manages to drop her slate and break it. Whoops.
- Mr. Brocklehurst gives Jane a new slate and dries her tears ...OK, OK, we're lying again. You can see where this is going, though. Jane gets called up front and made to stand on a stool in front of everyone while Mr. Brocklehurst goes off about what a careless, evil, lying, heathen, demon child she is. Really. We're glad he can get his kicks from mocking

ten-year-old girls, because otherwise he would probably have to steal candy from babies or something.

- Mr. Brocklehurst sweeps out, *very* pleased with himself, ordering that Jane stay on her stool in front of everyone for the rest of the day, and forbids anyone to speak to her.
- Jane's completely mortified, but her friend Helen makes an excuse to pass by her a few times and smiles at her. The smiles are all that keep Jane going.

Volume I, Chapter Eight

- The school day finally ends, the pupils go out to have their early evening meal (they call it tea), and Jane lets herself fall off the stool she's been standing on, curl up on the ground, and cry. She thinks all her hopes of being a successful student at Lowood, of having any friends, or having any of the teachers on her side are completely dashed.
- Helen brings Jane something to eat and gently sets her right about a few things: everyone in the school knows what a hypocrite Mr. Brocklehurst is, and they're not going to despise Jane just because he doesn't like her. In fact, they might even be nicer to her secretly because they know how unfair he is and they all hate him.
- Helen also says that, even if everyone hated Jane, if she knew herself to be innocent, that would be enough (because, we gather, God would be on her side). Jane's not so sure about this; she doesn't think she could live without friends.
- Helen starts talking about the rewards of the afterlife, and Jane feels melancholy – she's not sure why. And Helen starts coughing ominously! Da-da-da-dum. Guess what's going to happen to her pretty soon?
- Miss Temple comes and takes Jane and Helen to her room (sort of like going to the principal's office). But they're not in trouble – Miss Temple just wants to check on Jane and see how she's feeling after being humiliated in front of everyone.
- Miss Temple asks Jane for her own version of her life story, and Jane tells her side of things about Mrs. Reed and Gateshead. Jane realizes how important it is to tell the exact truth here, and so she doesn't embroider the story at all.
- Luckily for Jane, Miss Temple knows Mr. Lloyd, and writes to him to corroborate Jane's story. She promises that, if he does, she won't treat Jane like a liar, no matter what that awful Mr. Brocklehurst says.
- Miss Temple checks on Helen: How is she feeling? How's her cough? What's her pulse like? Da-da-da-dum.
- Helen and Jane get to have tea and seed-cake with Miss Temple. It's not much, but hey, it's not burned porridge, either.
- Jane listens as Miss Temple and Helen have a sparkling conversation about all sorts of things; both of them are well-read and intelligent and know a lot about a lot of things, and Jane doesn't know half as much. She'd like to, though!
- Jane and Helen go back to the large, dormitory-style bedroom, and, of course, something unpleasant happens to spoil their evening. Miss Scatcherd has just gone through Helen's drawers and is going to punish her for being messy.
- The next day, Miss Scatcherd makes Helen wear a sign that says "Slattern" tied to her forehead for the day. Jane feels terrible on Helen's behalf, but Helen, as usual, is a

patient, sweet-natured martyr about everything. Did we say *martyr*? Da-da-da-dum!
- Mr. Lloyd answers Miss Temple's letter and confirms the story that Jane told. Jane feels freed up to concentrate on her schoolwork and begins to do really well in all her classes. She's almost happy at Lowood these days. (Uh-oh!)

Volume I, Chapter Nine

- Things get a little bit better at Lowood when winter dissolves into spring; not only is it warmer and more comfortable for the girls, but Jane also discovers how beautiful the landscape around the school really is, now that it isn't covered with snow and ice anymore. She even gets to wander around in the woods alone enjoying herself. By herself? That's the catch.
- Spring may be warmer and prettier at Lowood, but it's also unhealthy. After all, the girls are already half-starved, and they've had colds and other winter illnesses; now that the stream and forest are damp and warm, they start catching typhus, and soon it's practically an epidemic.
- [Wait a minute, we can hear you saying: they get sick because it's misty? What's all this about "fog and fog-bred pestilence" (1.9.5)? That's not something they covered in your biology class, is it? Well, here's the thing: contagious disease wasn't completely understood in the nineteenth century, and one theory (known as "the miasma theory") was that fogs and air currents and so forth caused disease. Later in the century scientists confirmed the existence of microorganisms (known to you as "germs," or "the what's-really-going-on theory").]
- Anyway, whatever the reason, more than half the girls are sick, many die, and they can't run the school and classes as usual.
- The beautiful natural landscape and blooming flowers outside contrasts strangely with the disease and death inside the school.
- Jane, luckily, remains healthy, and pretty much gets to do whatever she wants while everyone else is busy being sick or tending to the sick.
- There is one bonus: the Brocklehursts are too afraid to visit the school, so at least all this isn't made worse by their self-righteous hypocrisy. Now *that's* a silver lining, sort of. The girls get to eat larger portions and things are generally nicer – except for the whole lots-of-people-dying thing.
- Jane's new best friend is a girl called Mary Ann Wilson, who is a little older than her and can tell her lots of "amusing stories" and "racy and pungent gossip" (1.9.10). Jane admits that Mary Ann isn't anywhere near as wonderful as Helen Burns, but unfortunately Helen is sick and confined to her bed.
- Unlike the other sick girls, Helen doesn't have typhus – she has consumption (which is the nineteenth-century name for tuberculosis). Jane doesn't really understand what consumption is, and she thinks Helen is going to be OK, so she doesn't worry about it too much.
- One evening Jane and Mary Ann get lost and return to Lowood late at night to find the surgeon, Mr. Bates, is at the house. Mary Ann goes in, but Jane stays outside to plant some things in her garden that she collected in the woods.

- While outside, Jane starts to realize how terrible death and mortality really are, and how incomprehensible the leap into the next world is.
- Jane's thoughts are interrupted by Mr. Bates and a nurse coming out; she asks the nurse about Helen Burns, and learns that Helen is dying. She tells Jane that she can't see her, either.
- Jane goes to bed, but can't sleep. She sneaks out of the bedroom to Miss Temple's room, where Helen has been lying sick.
- Jane creeps past the nurse quietly and is able to speak to Helen. She can't believe how calm Helen is in the face of death.
- Helen asks Jane to lie in the bed and cuddle with her to stay warm while they talk. While Jane snuggles warmly beside her, she explains that she thinks her death is fortunate: everyone dies, and at least her death is quiet and comfortable. She doesn't think she would have done well in the world, anyway, and she has faith in God's love. Helen is so perfect we could just scream, but Jane is comforted by her.
- Jane and Helen fall asleep, and Jane wakes up being carried back to her own bed. It's not until two days later that she finds out Helen died that night, with Jane's arms around her neck. That is *so creepy*. And it's not like we had any hints that Helen was going to die young or anything.

Volume I, Chapter Ten

- The older Jane narrating the novel breaks in, explaining that she's going to skip eight years ahead in the story. First, she fills us in on a few details of what's happened at Lowood in the meantime:
- Many girls died of typhus at the school, but the outbreak put the school in the public eye, and Mr. Brocklehurst's cruelty and neglect as an inspector became known. Other people who had both money and compassion got involved, built a new school building in a better place, and passed new regulations to make the school more humane.
- Mr. Brocklehurst is still treasurer, but there are other people looking over his shoulder now, if you know what we mean, to make sure the girls have enough to eat and nobody cuts their hair off for them or anything weird and cruel like that.
- Jane is a student at the school for six more years and then becomes a teacher there for two years.
- At this point, Miss Temple, who has been Jane's mentor and inspiration and all that jazz, gets married and leaves the school.
- Jane realizes that, without Miss Temple, she's not content to stay at Lowood anymore – she wants to get out in the world and have adventures! She looks out her window at the road to the school and realizes she hasn't traveled away from the school on that road at all since she arrived there eight years ago. Even if her new adventure is just a new lowly position somewhere else, she wants to get away.
- Jane's longing for freedom is interrupted by her teaching duties. Finally, after her teacher-roommate Miss Gryce falls asleep that night, she can start thinking again about how to leave Lowood.
- Jane decides to advertise herself in the regional newspaper as an available tutor or

governess. She posts the ad without telling anyone at Lowood what she's doing.

- A week later, Jane goes into town to see if any letters came in response to her ad; everyone at Lowood thinks she's going "to get measured for a pair of shoes" (1.10.26). There is one letter, but she has to wait for that evening, after everyone is asleep, to read it.
- Jane is satisfied with the situation offered by the letter, which is a post as governess to a little girl less than ten years old. The salary is double what she makes at Lowood. She's also glad that the letter writer is an older woman, a Mrs. Fairfax, and she imagines Mrs. Fairfax as an elderly widow with one daughter at her home – Thornfield.
- Jane tells the current superintendent of the school about her new job and asks her to be the one to tell Mr. Brocklehurst so that she doesn't have to talk to him herself. He insists on writing to Mrs. Reed, but she doesn't care at all and says Jane can do whatever she wants.
- Jane gets everything prepared over the next two weeks. As she is waiting for the carriage to come to take her on the first part of her journey to Thornfield, someone comes to see her – Bessie!
- Bessie tells Jane all the news about Gateshead. Bessie and Robert Leaven, the coachman, are married, and Bessie has a three-year-old boy, who is with her on the visit to see Jane. Georgiana Reed is curvy, stout, and pretty, and tried to elope with a lord. Eliza Reed is tall, thin, and jealous of her sister's romance. John has flunked out of college, failed to become a barrister, and is generally a good-for-nothing, spending his mom's money. Mrs. Reed is upset about John's conduct.
- Bessie exults over Jane's achievements at school – her piano playing, painting, French, and sewing are far superior to the Reed girls' abilities. Even so, Bessie is honest with Jane about her looks – she is "no beauty" but she does "look like a lady" (1.10.64).
- Bessie also tells Jane that one of her relatives, possibly her uncle, came to Gateshead to see her seven years ago, but had to leave for Madeira before he could go to Lowood to see her. They speculate that he may be a wine merchant or employed by one.
- Bessie leaves to go back to Gateshead, and Jane leaves for Thornfield.

Volume I, Chapter Eleven

- Jane stages the beginning of the next chapter almost like a play, describing the scene as she sits by the fire at an inn, waiting nervously to get to Thornfield and meet this mysterious Mrs. Fairfax and her daughter. (She's *assuming* the little girl is Mrs. Fairfax's daughter.)
- Notice that Jane (or perhaps Charlotte Brontë) addresses the reader directly here, something that happens only a few times in the novel, but always at key points (see, for example, the beginning of Book I, Chapter Ten and the beginning of Book III, Chapter Twelve).
- A servant meets Jane and drives her in a coach to Thornfield. Jane guesses that his plain clothes mean that Mrs. Fairfax isn't too wealthy. It's amazing, in fact, how little Jane knows about the job that she's heading into. We hope you would never take some random job based on one letter from someone you didn't know and then travel across the country alone to live who-knows-where.

- Jane arrives at Thornfield and is brought in to see Mrs. Fairfax, who looks almost exactly as she had expected; she's an old woman dressed in black clothes and a widow's cap, which probably means she's mourning her husband.
- Jane is surprised that Mrs. Fairfax welcomes her kindly, chatting with her and offering her tea; she's never been treated so politely by anyone, especially an employer. She's really relieved that this situation is better than her previous ones.
- Suddenly, a surprise: Jane finds out that her new student isn't Mrs. Fairfax's daughter; her name is Miss Varens, and Mrs. Fairfax doesn't have any kids. Unfortunately, Jane is too shy to ask more about Miss Varens at this point.
- Mrs. Fairfax tells Jane more about the household; it's been somewhat lonely for her, because she can't socialize with the maid, Leah, or the other servants, who are a married couple. Jane, however, will be closer to Mrs. Fairfax's "level," whatever that is.
- Jane goes to bed; her room is small but nice, and she feels very secure in it...although the long, dark corridors of the house are, she admits, a little bit creepy.
- Jane wakes up on her first day at Thornfield, soothed by the luxurious surroundings, and dresses in her plain Lowood-style clothes and heads downstairs. She meets Mrs. Fairfax again and learns that the owner of Thornfield is a Mr. Rochester – Mrs. Fairfax is just the housekeeper, although she is a distant cousin of Rochester's. Adèle, Mrs. Fairfax explains, is Mr. Rochester's ward.
- Jane meets Adèle, a French girl about seven or eight years old who only speaks a little English. It's lucky that Jane learned French from a native speaker; she's able to understand Adèle easily, even when Adèle talks really fast.
- Adèle tells Jane (and Jane relays to Mrs. Fairfax) how she came to England about six months ago. Long before that, the first thing Adèle remembers is living with her mother, who taught her to sing and dance and had a lot of, erm, let's call them gentlemen admirers. There were ladies who liked to hear Madame Varens sing, too, but there seem to have been quite a few gentlemen, as well, if you take our meaning.
- Adèle offers to sing for Jane, and sings a song from an opera that's really far too mature for her. The contrast between Adèle's childishness and the extremes of jealousy and passion in the song seems crass to Jane. Then Adèle recites a poem with similar strange adult motifs and techniques. Jane's pretty weirded out by her and stops her before she can dance.
- Jane questions Adèle further about her history; Adèle explains that, after her mother died, Mr. Rochester offered to take her with him to live in England, and (as she explained earlier) she and her nurse Sophie came with him on a steamship across the (English) Channel. Unfortunately, Mr. Rochester took her to Thornfield, left her there, and went traveling, so Adèle doesn't actually get to live with him.
- Jane teaches Adèle her first lesson that morning; Adèle is obedient, but not very studious. She's never really been asked to apply herself. Jane decides to take it slow and lets her have the afternoon free.
- In the afternoon, Jane talks to Mrs. Fairfax about Thornfield and Mr. Rochester while Mrs. Fairfax does some light housework. Jane is amazed at how beautiful and fancy the house is.
- Jane practically cross-examines Mrs. Fairfax about the absent Mr. Rochester. She really wants to know what kind of a person he is, but it's hard for the housekeeper to describe him. Most people like him, she tells Jane, but he is "rather peculiar," whatever that means (1.11.99).

- Jane follows Mrs. Fairfax through the house, admiring everything she sees, but feeling a little creeped out by all the empty rooms full of strange furnishings and decorations. She asks Mrs. Fairfax if there are any ghost stories about Thornfield, but there aren't. However, Mrs. Fairfax does admit that the members of the Rochester family have been "rather a violent than a quiet race in their time" (1.11.109). So there may not be any ghosts...but there are some metaphorical skeletons in the closet.
- Jane and Mrs. Fairfax make their way to the attic and then to the roof, and Jane is able to look out across all of the land surrounding Thornfield, which is an incredible view.
- After a good long look, they head back; Mrs. Fairfax is fastening the trap door and Jane is a bit further away in the attic when she hears an eerie, unearthly laugh. Mrs. Fairfax says that it must be one of the servants, perhaps a woman named Grace Poole who does the sewing.
- Jane's convinced there is no Grace and that the laugh is a ghost, but at Mrs. Fairfax's call Grace comes out of a room nearby. She's a squat, heavyset, middle-aged redhead – SO not a ghost. Mrs. Fairfax tells her there should be less noise, sends her off, and changes the subject. Sure, THAT'S not suspicious at all.

Volume I, Chapter Twelve

- Jane continues to work as Adèle's governess; her life with Mrs. Fairfax and her pupil is much more pleasant than anything she's experienced before, but she's still restless for adventure and excitement, or at least some contact with the outside world. Her favorite activity is going up to the roof of Thornfield and looking across the landscape.
- Jane defends her dissatisfaction to the reader: she knows that many will think she should be happy with what she has, but she thinks everyone, including women, needs "exercise for their faculties" (1.12.5).
- When she's up on the roof or in the attic, Jane often hears Grace Poole's weird laugh, but she's never able to draw Grace into a real conversation.
- Jane tells us that her relationships with the other servants are good, but not especially exciting.
- Three months go by, and now it's January. Jane decides to give Adèle a holiday and volunteers to take a long walk and carry a letter for Mrs. Fairfax two miles to the nearby town of Hay.
- Jane enjoys the walk, despite the cold weather, and takes delight in the beautiful landscape around her. She stops partway along the lane and sits on a stile, examining her surroundings. Suddenly, she hears a horse coming, and she stays on the stile, sitting quietly, to let it pass.
- While she's waiting for the horse to go by, Jane suddenly remembers the spooky stories Bessie used to tell her about a spirit called a "Gytrash," which could appear as a horse or dog to lost or lonely travelers. And then – a dog comes around the corner, looking exactly as Bessie described the Gytrash. But when the horse appears, the fact that it has a rider breaks the spell; the Gytrash never has a rider or a companion. (Hmm, who could this mysterious rider be?)
- The horse and rider pass, and Jane starts to go on her way, but then she hears the horse

slip on the ice, and horse and rider both fall. The dog runs about, trying to help, and finally runs over to Jane – she must be the only other person for a mile all around.

- Jane helps the gentleman up; he has sprained his ankle, but is mostly OK. He is thirty-five, dark and stern; Jane explains that, if he had been a handsome young man, she would have recoiled from him, but she's able to approach him as he is.
- Jane insists on helping him, and he questions her about who she is; she explains that she's the governess in Mr. Rochester's household. He seems a bit surprised by this, but doesn't explain who he is. (Who is he, anyway?) We do learn that the dog's name is Pilot, but that's not much help.
- Unfortunately, Jane's not able to catch the bridle of the spooked horse, so instead she helps the man over to the horse and lets him lean on her to remount; then they go their separate ways. We'll probably never see him again, right?
- After delivering the letter in the town, Jane walks back to Thornfield, pleased to have helped someone, and interested in the man she met. She's a bit disappointed to go back home to her boring old existence. She loiters outside for a long time, looking at the sky, reluctant to go inside.
- When she finally re-enters Thornfield, she hears voices in the dining room. She looks for Mrs. Fairfax, but finds Pilot instead. Jane calls the maid and learns that the master of the house has just arrived with a sprained ankle. That's right – that stranger in the lane was *Mr. Rochester*. Are you shocked? Nah, we didn't think so. Jane's a bit out of the loop, though, isn't she?

Volume I, Chapter Thirteen

- Jane doesn't see Mr. Rochester again that evening – he's in bed with his sprained ankle. She and Adèle continue their lessons in a new upstairs room, instead of the library, where Mr. Rochester is conducting business. Jane's excited about all the new activity in the household, all the people coming and going to see Mr. Rochester – the place is coming alive, and she prefers it that way.
- Adèle is having a lot of trouble concentrating when she knows Mr. Rochester is downstairs – she keeps trying to sneak downstairs to see him or to guess what presents he might have brought her. Adèle tells Jane that Mr. Rochester has been asking about her – especially what she looks like.
- In the early evening, Mr. Rochester invites Jane and Adèle to have tea with him. Jane changes into her second-best dress, which is almost as plain as her regular dress, and puts on her only piece of jewelry, a simple pearl pin.
- As soon as she comes into the dining room, Jane recognizes Mr. Rochester as, of course, the stranger whom she helped after his horse slipped on the ice.
- Mr. Rochester is once again somewhat rude to Jane, or at least abrupt and preoccupied, but she prefers that to flattery and polished manners. Jane thinks it's more interesting this way.
- As Jane gives Rochester his teacup (he's lying down on a couch because of his sprained ankle), Adèle asks him if he has a present for Jane. He starts asking Jane whether she likes presents, and her subtle but saucy replies draw his interest. When he complements

her on how much she's taught Adèle, she claims that that's the best gift she could have. Aww, how sweet.

- Mr. Rochester asks Jane about her past history; when he hears that she was at Lowood for eight years, he says that must be why she looks so eerie and unworldly. He compares her to the fairies and sprites of the wood, and suggests that she bewitched his horse to make it fall the day before. Mrs. Fairfax, who doesn't get the joke, is confused, but we're sure that *you* know just how serious Rochester actually is.
- Rochester keeps quizzing Jane about her background: she has no immediate family, came to Thornfield by answering Mrs. Fairfax's ad, has never lived in a town or known many people, and has only read the few books that were available to her here and there. She sounds pretty green, really.
- Once again Jane surprises Rochester, this time by being harsh and honest about Mr. Brocklehurst.
- Next Rochester examines Jane's various achievements, listening to her play the piano and examining her sketches. He, like Jane, is harsh and honest about the merits of her work; her piano playing, he says, is OK, but some of her sketches and paintings seem to really impress him – three of them in particular.
- The three of Jane's watercolors that Rochester finds really fascinating are each of landscapes that she painted from her imagination; one is of a stormy sea and a shipwreck with a corpse, one of a grassy hill with the Evening Star personified as a shadowy woman, and one is of an icy arctic scene with a strange, pale, despairing figure in the foreground.
- Jane admits to Rochester that she enjoyed painting these images, but that she was "tormented by the contrast" (1.13.115) between what she was actually able to paint and what she saw in her head.
- Rochester tells Jane that her paintings are intriguing and strange, but that she's not an artistic master. He keeps getting drawn in by the images, though, and seems to think that she's managed to paint real places without knowing it.
- Suddenly, Rochester sends Jane off to put Adèle to bed, and retires for the night himself.
- Jane talks with Mrs. Fairfax about Rochester, who is far stranger than the housekeeper previously implied. Mrs. Fairfax tells Jane that they should make allowances for him because of his family problems: his elder brother died nine years before, and then he inherited the estate.
- Apparently, there was some sort of problem between the current Mr. Rochester, whose name is Edward; his brother, Rowland Rochester; and his father, Old Mr. Rochester. Old Mr. Rochester and Rowland put Edward in a bad position so that he would make money, but it's unclear what exactly happened.
- Now that his father and brother are gone, Mr. Edward Rochester tends to stay away from Thornfield and only visit it for short periods, perhaps because of bad memories. Da-DUM! A mystery!

Volume I, Chapter Fourteen

- For a little while, Jane doesn't see Rochester much; he has a lot of business and goes out riding frequently. Sometimes he is haughty or cold, but she can tell that he's just moody, and that his attitude doesn't really have anything to do with her.

- One evening, Rochester sends for Jane and Adèle after dinner. A box of presents that Rochester has bought for Adèle has arrived, and he parks her in the corner with it, exactly the way some parents might park a kid in the corner with the TV to keep them busy. He calls in Mrs. Fairfax, so that Adèle can talk to her about the presents while he talks to Jane.
- Rochester keeps insisting that Jane bring her chair closer to him instead of moving back into the shadows so that he can't see her face. He seems to be in a better mood than usual, but he's still not very good at being polite; he tends to order her around.
- Suddenly, because she is staring at him, Rochester asks Jane if she thinks he's handsome. Without thinking, she gives an honest answer: No.
- Jane's immediately sorry that she didn't say something more socially acceptable, like "Beauty is in the eye of the beholder," but Rochester doesn't seem to mind – in fact, he seems glad that she's honest.
- He asks her to criticize him, and she examines his skull and face. (This is more weird nineteenth-century pseudo-science: it was a common belief in the Victorian period that you could determine someone's character from the shape of their skull. The technical name for this is "phrenology.") Based on the shape of Rochester's skull, Jane suggests that he might not be very charitable – and, from his reaction, she's absolutely right.
- Rochester explains a little bit about himself, suggesting that, when he was younger, he used to give people the benefit of the doubt, but these days he's pretty jaded. He asks Jane if she thinks he can turn back into "flesh," (i.e., into his old self) but she doesn't know enough about his past to make the call. He's glad, however, that he confused her, because it keeps her from staring piercingly at his face. This is really heating up! Too bad he's almost twice her age (remember, she's 18, he's 35).
- Jane continues to think about Rochester's appearance; she thinks that a lot of people might find him ugly, but something about the way he carries himself makes him imposing.
- Rochester tells her that he's feeling chatty tonight, and orders Jane to chat with him about something. He's really not very good at this small-talk stuff. Jane doesn't know what he likes to talk about, so she doesn't say anything.
- Rochester tries to explain his attitude toward Jane a little; even though he's kind of abrupt and tends to order her to do things instead of asking, he doesn't want to treat her as an inferior. At least, he explains, he only considers himself her superior because he's so much older and more experienced than she is. And so he will sometimes order her around and be "masterful," he says, but she'll have to forgive him.
- Jane contradicts him: just because he's older and has done more doesn't mean he's wiser, she tells him. It depends on what he's done with those seventeen years he has over on her; maybe he hasn't learned anything. He has to admit that she's right, but he still wants to be able to order her around sometimes, and tries to think of an excuse.
- Jane smiles at this – after all, he's paying her to take his orders, which he seems to have forgotten. She reminds him, and he leaps on this: will she agree to let him order her around a bit because she's getting paid?
- No, Jane says, getting paid isn't enough, but she will let him order her around simply because he was worried about her feelings and wanted her to be comfortable with how he treated her.
- Rochester presses the point: is it OK if he drops a lot of the polite nonsense? She won't just think he's being rude? Jane's a bit careful on this point; she's OK with him being informal, but not with him actually being a jerk. No salary would make up, she says, for

actually being treated badly.

- Rochester thinks that a lot of people don't have Jane's principles and would let themselves get mistreated for money, but he's impressed with her answers, her tendency to stand up for herself, and her strong personality.
- Then Rochester changes his mind a little: Jane is unusual, he says, but maybe she has flaws that make up for her good points. Jane doesn't say anything, but it's clear that she's thinking the same thing about him.
- Rochester admits that he has a checkered past, but a lot of it he blames on the circumstances. Again, Jane doesn't know – and *we* don't yet know – exactly what he's talking about, but it sounds pretty sordid...and really interesting.
- Next Rochester tells Jane that one of her major roles in life is to listen. Did you ever have that one friend who somehow gets to hear everybody's personal problems? Like, they don't really ask, but something makes everyone tell that particular person everything? Rochester thinks Jane is going to be one of those people – but maybe he's just making excuses for having told her so much already.
- Rochester talks about remorse and regretting his past mistakes, whatever those are. Jane advises him to repent, and Rochester says that reform is better than repentance, but that there's something standing in the way of his reform.
- Jane says he'll just get worse and worse if he keeps grabbing for pleasure without changing, and that eventually his pleasures will sour anyway. He doesn't like being preached to and objects to this, but, Jane holds her ground.
- Now Rochester tries to claim that the "temptation" he is feeling is actually an "inspiration," that it's an angel and not a devil. We're going crazy to know what the heck it is he's tempted to do. Jane tells him that it's still a temptation, no matter what he says, and he should resist.
- Rochester gets a bit over-excited here and dramatically mimes taking the "angel" or "demon" or whatever this idea is into himself. Jane's really confused at this point, but insists that, if Rochester feels like he's not a good person, that he should make a genuine effort to change.
- Rochester tells Jane that he *is* going to change, and that, if what he's doing is immoral, then he'll declare a new moral law to make it right. Jane claims that anything that needs morals to change in order to be OK is obviously immoral.
- They argue about ethics for a bit, and Jane keeps getting the better of him. Basically, Rochester really wants to do something, we don't know what, and Jane can tell from how he talks about it that it's wrong, even though she doesn't know what it is or why.
- Jane ends the conversation by getting up and going to put Adèle to bed. Rochester is worried that he drove her away by saying such weird things, but she assures him that she's not afraid of him, even though she is a little confused.
- Rochester discerns that Jane isn't naturally so stern and repressed – it's the effect of Lowood, he says, and it will wear off. He describes her as a caged bird that wants to be free. She doesn't really say anything to this, but it seems a lot like how she described herself at the beginning of the last chapter.
- While Jane and Rochester have been talking, Adèle has run out to try on one of the dresses that were among her new presents from Rochester. When she comes back and frolics around in the dress, she looks just like her mother.
- Rochester hints at his involvement with Adèle's mother – Céline Varens. It's not clear yet what Rochester's actual relationship to Adèle is – but if he was "involved" with her mother,

then we can guess that maybe he's ...yeah, you got it.

Volume I, Chapter Fifteen

- One day, while Rochester and Jane are walking in the garden outside Thornfield, Rochester explains his relationship to Adèle's mother, Céline Varens, more explicitly. It's a pretty exciting story, so sit back as Rochester begins his tale:
- Céline was a French opera-dancer with whom Rochester fell in love – and he *thought* she loved him, too.
- Rochester became Céline's sugar daddy – he paid for her to live in an expensive hotel, have lots of servants, and every possible luxury. In fact, all this was almost too expensive even for the wealthy Rochester, and he was well on the way to spending his whole fortune on her.
- One evening, Rochester went to Céline's place and she was out, so he sat on the balcony waiting for her. He saw her come back to the hotel in the carriage he was paying for – with another guy.
- Rochester breaks into his own story to comment on the way jealousy poisons everything – for a long time he even hated being at Thornfield because...he stops before telling us why.
- There's a long pause while Rochester and Jane stroll along the path and Rochester seems to be wrestling with himself. He tells Jane that he is fighting with a witchy specter of his destiny, and that now he's defying her and daring to enjoy being at Thornfield.
- Adèle comes close to Rochester and Jane as she's playing, and Rochester orders her away. Jane prompts him to continue his story.
- Before Rochester continues, he notes again how strange it is that he's telling all this to Jane – what kind of guy tells his 18-year-old employee about his sordid affair with a French mistress? But he knows, he says, that Jane is made to be a confidante, and that what he's telling her won't hurt her and may help him. Then he continues the story:
- Rochester stayed hidden on the balcony behind the curtains, waiting for Céline and her lover to come in.
- Céline and the other guy entered, and Rochester stopped being jealous – because the guy was a cruel idiot Rochester has met before. Rochester decided right away that Céline wasn't worth his time if she would have an affair with such a loser.
- Rochester continued to hide and listen to them, but was mostly bored by their lame conversation. He was a bit irritated when they started insulting him behind his back, especially because Céline used to complement him to his face constantly. (That's why he was so glad Jane was honest about his looks.)
- Adèle runs up and interrupts the story, saying that someone has come to see Mr. Rochester. Rochester quickly finishes the story for Jane:
- Rochester walked in, turned Céline out in the street with a little money to see her through the next few days, and arranged a duel with the lover the next day, at which he shot the guy in the arm. And that was that...
- ...but Rochester couldn't just wash his hands of the whole thing because, six months earlier, Céline had given birth to Adèle. She claimed that Adèle was Rochester's daughter; he doesn't think so, but she could be. (We think they should go on *Geraldo*.)

- Several years later, Céline abandoned Adèle and ran off to Italy with another guy.
- Rochester still didn't think Adèle was his daughter (or so he claims to Jane), but he felt sorry for her and brought her back to England to grow up under better circumstances.
- Having finished the story, Rochester asks Jane if now she feels differently about her job as Adèle's governess. Jane answers that she cares even more about the girl now that she knows Adèle is practically an orphan.
- Rochester goes in, and Jane stays outside playing with her pupil and the dog. She is more tender to Adèle after hearing the story.
- That evening, as she's going to sleep, Jane thinks about what Rochester told her. Most of the story, she decides, is common enough, but the moment where Rochester freaked out while thinking about Thornfield still seems weird. Still, she can't explain it, so she starts thinking about something else – how Rochester treats her.
- Jane's glad that Rochester trusts her so much and that he always seems pleased to see her. He still does most of the talking when they're together, but she likes to learn from him and respond to his thoughts. She feels like they're family, not master and servant.
- Jane decides that Rochester has it in him to be a good person and hopes that she can help him deal with his past, whatever it might be.
- And Jane wonders – a bit ominously, we think – how long he'll be able to stay at Thornfield before whatever it is that he hates about the place crops up again. She knows she'll really regret it if he leaves.
- Lying awake in bed worrying, Jane hears something strange. She tries to tell herself that it's nothing, but then she hears the demonic laugh that usually comes from the attic. Someone is outside her bedroom door!
- Jane gets up, locks the door, and demands to know who's there. There's no answer, but she hears footsteps walking away.
- Determined to talk to Mrs. Fairfax, Jane unbolts the door and leaves the room – only to discover a lit candle sitting outside her door and the hallway filled with smoke. The door to Mr. Rochester's room is open, and the smoke is billowing out of it.
- Hardly thinking, Jane runs into Rochester's room, where she finds the bed curtains on fire. She tries to shake Rochester awake, but he's already half unconscious from inhaling the smoke, so she's forced to throw a nearby basin of water over him. She manages to put out most of the fire and wake him up.
- Rochester's first reaction is to swear, and his second one is to call Jane a fairy and a sorceress.
- Jane runs to get the candle from the hall, and she and Rochester look at the wet, scorched bed. She tells him about the laugh she heard and how she came to find him there.
- Strangely, Rochester's not surprised – just worried. Jane asks if she should call Mrs. Fairfax or someone else, but Rochester instructs her to stay in his room alone while he goes up to the third floor with the candle.
- After a long time, while Jane sits in the dark waiting for him, Rochester comes back and says that it's just what he thought happened – but he doesn't explain this thought to Jane.
- Rochester makes sure that Jane didn't see anything, and then accepts her theory that it is the seamstress Grace Poole who caused the damage. He tells Jane to say nothing about the whole incident.
- When Jane starts to leave, Rochester stops her, takes her hand, and thanks her for saving his life. He seems to want to say something else...but he doesn't...and he won't let go of her hand!

- Eventually, Jane convinces Rochester that she has to leave before Mrs. Fairfax comes, and he releases her. Jane goes back to bed, but, unsurprisingly, she can't sleep.

Volume II, Chapter One

- Jane is convinced that Rochester will come and visit her and Adèle in the schoolroom the next day, but he doesn't.
- She overhears the other servants talking – they are under the impression that Rochester was sleeping with a lit candle beside his bed, woke up with the bed on fire, and put it out himself. None of them know about Jane's involvement or about the strange visit from someone on the third floor.
- When she passes Rochester's bedroom, Jane sees Grace Poole sitting beside the bed, sewing new curtains. She can't believe that Grace is just sitting there, behaving normally, and she questions the servant about the incident to trick her into betraying her guilt.
- Grace doesn't seem guilty, but she does seem to know something, and asks if Jane heard anything last night.
- Jane tells Grace about the eerie laugh, insisting that she wasn't dreaming. Grace asks if she saw anything, and Jane tells her that instead of looking outside, she locked her door – which is true, although she went outside a little later.
- Grace advises Jane to keep her door locked every night – which Jane takes as either hypocrisy about safety, or a weird threat.
- Jane tries to figure out why Rochester has insisted that she keep the events of the night a secret, and what power Grace Poole could have over him to prevent him from having her arrested, or at least firing her, after she tried to murder him in his bed.
- She briefly speculates that perhaps Grace is Mr. Rochester's ex-lover, and that he has to do what she says so that she doesn't expose him, but she can't quite believe this – Grace is so plain-looking and matronly, almost ugly, and they just don't seem to be a match. Of course, Rochester seems to like Jane, and she's no looker, so maybe it could be true.
- Jane reminds herself that even if she's not pretty, she is ladylike, which Grace isn't, and then she trembles, remembering Rochester's behavior the night before. She's teaching Adèle at the moment, and the girl notices her daydreaming.
- That evening, Jane expects Rochester to send for her so that they can talk further about the murder attempt, but when she goes downstairs to have tea with Mrs. Fairfax, she discovers that Rochester left right after breakfast to stay with some friends ten miles away at a house called "the Leas." Mrs. Fairfax thinks he will stay there for a week.
- Jane's first question is whether there are any ladies at the Leas – and there are several, including the local beauty, Blanche Ingram. Blanche, according to Mrs. Fairfax, is gorgeous and accomplished and sang duets with Mr. Rochester.
- Jane suggests to Mrs. Fairfax that Rochester might be interested in marrying Blanche Ingram. Mrs. Fairfax thinks the age difference is too much – Blanche is only twenty-five. Jane's about to push the issue, but Adèle comes in and they have to start talking about something else.
- Later, alone in her room, Jane kicks herself for being such an idiot and thinking that Rochester would actually be interested in her.

- Jane decides that, the next day, she will make two sketches, one of herself with all her flaws, and one of a beautiful woman who fits the description Mrs. Fairfax gave of Blanche Ingram. Whenever she starts to think of Mr. Rochester fondly, she'll compare these two portraits, and remind herself that she can't compete with women like Blanche. Doesn't that sound healthy?
- The next morning, she spends an hour or two drawing her own portrait, and two weeks making one of her imagined version of Blanche.

Volume II, Chapter Two

- For a week, Jane doesn't hear anything about what Rochester's doing; she tries to discipline herself and stop thinking about it, but she can't. She starts wondering if she should quit her job as Adèle's governess and get a new one somewhere else.
- After another week (so now two weeks have gone by since the fire and Rochester's sudden departure), Mrs. Fairfax receives a letter from Rochester telling her that he's coming back to Thornfield in a few days with a bunch of friends.
- Everyone spends the three days making frantic preparations for all the guests – except Adèle, who is an absolute pest and keeps getting underfoot.
- Jane is also helping Mr. Fairfax get the house ready for everyone, which is why Adèle has nothing better to do than flounce around being obnoxious.
- When Jane isn't busy working, she wonders what's going on with Grace Poole, who spends almost all her time alone on the third floor and doesn't help anyone with anything.
- Jane overhears a conversation between one of the maids, Leah, and another servant, a charwoman (house cleaner). Apparently Grace Poole gets paid more than anyone else at Thornfield, and Leah thinks that what Grace does for Mr. Rochester is well worth the money. Jane doesn't learn any more than that, because they notice her listening and stop talking. The charwoman is surprised that Jane doesn't know Thornfield's secret, but nobody seems to want to tell her.
- Finally it's Thursday, the day Mr. Rochester said he would arrive with his guests. Everyone puts on their nicest clothes and sits around waiting for them to arrive. When they finally ride up, some in carriages and some on horses, a beautiful woman in a purple dress is riding beside Rochester. It's Blanche Ingram!
- The visitors enter, and Jane sits with Adèle, half-listening to their noise and half trying to keep Adèle from running down and bothering them.
- The women come upstairs to change their clothes after the trip, and Jane sneaks downstairs to get something that she and Adèle can eat for dinner. She's not sneaking because she isn't supposed to have dinner – she's sneaking because she doesn't want anyone to see her.
- Unfortunately, Jane doesn't make it back upstairs before the ladies start coming down, so she has to stand still at the end of a dark hallway and hope they don't notice her.
- The women pass, and Jane and Adèle both feel pretty awed by their fancy clothes and even fancier attitudes. Jane, Adèle, and Adèle's nurse Sophie eat the food Jane's scrounged up in the kitchen, forgotten by pretty much everyone and listening a little to the bustle downstairs.

- Adèle can't sleep for all the noise and excitement, so Jane sits with her at the top of the stairs listening to the women play on the piano and to Blanche and Mr. Rochester singing duets. Eventually Adèle falls asleep and Jane puts her to bed.
- The party doesn't break up until one in the morning, and Jane still hasn't seen Rochester at all. He seems to have forgotten her completely.
- The next day, Rochester and his guests take advantage of the nice weather and go out riding to see something or other nearby, Jane doesn't know what. Jane watches them leave and come back from her window, noticing how Mr. Rochester and Blanche Ingram are riding together on their own, apart from everyone else.
- Mrs. Fairfax tells Jane that Mr. Rochester wants Adèle and Jane to come and socialize with everyone after dinner this evening. Jane tries to make an excuse, but Mrs. Fairfax tells her that Rochester insisted she come and that he said he would fetch her if she refused.
- Adèle shows her true prissy-princess colors and goes crazy getting herself ready when she hears that she's going to make an appearance at the party. She keeps Jane and Sophie busy getting her ready, and then Jane and Adèle go and wait in a the drawing room for the party to finish their dinner
- The guests finish eating and the ladies enter the drawing room; Jane curtseys to them, and some of them nod to her, while others pretty much ignore her. (The men are still in the dining room; it was traditional at formal Victorian dinner parties for the women to leave the table first, go to another room, and chat or read; the men stayed behind, drinking and talking separately. Then, when the men feel ready, they come and join the women.)
- Jane explains who the different women are. There are eight of them, four older women and four younger: Mrs. Eshton and her daughters Amy and Louisa; the Dowager Lady Ingram and her daughters Blanche and Mary; Lady Lynn; and Mrs. Colonel Dent. "Dowager" means that Lady Ingram is a widow, and "Mrs. Colonel" means that Mrs. Dent's husband is, you guessed it, a Colonel.
- We'll tell you now that most of these women are minor characters and aren't too important to the plot of the novel. Important points to notice:•
- The Dowager Lady Ingram reminds Jane of Mrs. Reed, which probably means she's just as spiteful and malicious.•
- Blanche is incredibly beautiful, and she looks just the way Mrs. Fairfax described her to Jane – which means that she looks like the portrait Jane drew of her without having seen her yet. Creepy.•
- Blanche is also really clever, but in a nasty *Mean Girls* way instead of a quiet dorky Jane Eyre way.•
- Jane decides that Blanche is "majestic" but possibly not Rochester's type.
- Adèle, in her usual bratty way, starts demanding attention from the ladies. A few of them start spoiling her and petting her and she's as happy as a pig in...um, let's just say she's being a little princess and loving it.
- After a little while, the gentlemen come in to join the ladies and everyone drinks coffee. There are six men, including Mr. Rochester; the others are Henry and Frederick Lynn, Colonel Dent, Mr. Eshton, and Lord Ingram. Henry and Frederick are Lady Lynn's sons; Colonel Dent, obviously, is Mrs. Colonel Dent's husband; Mr. Eshton is Mrs. Eshton's husband and the father of Amy and Louisa, and Lord Ingram is the Dowager Lady Ingram's son and the brother of Blanche and Mary. Got all that? Don't worry, it's not super-important. Just focus on Blanche and her mom. And Jane and Rochester, of course.
- As Mr. Rochester comes in, Jane tries to focus on her knitting (she's making a beaded silk

purse). She remembers the last moment she saw him, where he didn't want to let go of her hand and they were alone together, and wonders what's happened to change everything and make him so distant.

- When Jane's sure that Mr. Rochester isn't looking at her, she lets herself look up and stare at him. Even though he's not handsome in the usual way, she realizes that to her he's *waaay* hot. She also figures out something we've known for a few chapters now: despite her best efforts, she's in love with him.
- Jane compares Rochester to the other men in the room; even though most people would probably think they're more handsome than he is, she has different taste.
- Jane decides that she and Rochester are alike; they have more in common with each other than he does with anyone else in the room. They're kindred spirits. Still, she doesn't think he'll ever be interested in her – she's too far beneath him.
- Everyone pairs off to chat, and Blanche flirts with Rochester. Unfortunately, Blanche's idea of flirting is to talk about how "detestable" and "ridiculous" governesses are, basically insulting Jane right to her face (although she's talking to Rochester, not Jane).
- Blanche and her brother tell stories about how they (and, to a small extent, their sister Mary) used to torment their previous governesses. Let's see, who do they sound like? Where else in this novel have we seen a brother, two sisters, and a widowed mother who are all vicious and selfish? Hmm, sounds like John, Eliza, and Georgiana Reed and their mother, doesn't it?
- Some of the other women start talking about their experiences with their governesses, and Blanche changes the subject; she doesn't want anyone else to have a chance to say something clever. She asks Rochester to sing a duet with her.
- Before Blanche and Rochester begin singing, they banter about what sort of man Rochester is and Blanche hints that he's just the type of man she wants for a husband: an ugly guy who worships her, instead of someone as handsome as she is. Nudge, nudge, Edward!
- Blanche and Rochester sing, and Jane wants to leave, but she's mesmerized by Rochester's voice. As soon as he finishes, she slips out into the hallway, but she has to stop and retie her sandal.
- Rochester comes out after Jane and asks why she didn't come and talk to him in the drawing room. He wants her to come back, but he can tell she's about to cry, so he lets her go – but first he insists that she join the party every night while they're there. He stops *just* short of calling her by some term of endearment – and then leaves.

Volume II, Chapter Three

- The party at Thornfield continues; things are much more active than they were during the first three months Jane spent there.
- One evening, the guests play charades, but it's a much more elaborate version of charades than we play these days, complete with costumes and teams of people working together to act out just one word or phrase.
- Rochester invites Jane to play, but she won't; she does watch, though.
- Blanche and Rochester team up and go first; they think up a phrase, and then put together

costumes and silent actions to act out the parts of the phrase. The phrase they choose has two parts.

- The first part of the phrase is the word "bride," and Rochester and Blanche pretend to be a couple getting married, wearing costumes and everything. We're sure Jane's not too happy to see their wedding, even if it is just a joke – this time.
- The second part of the phrase is harder for everyone to guess. Rochester and Blanche act out a complicated Biblical scene in which Rebecca gives Isaac a drink at the well of Nahor. Basically, this is a lot like the first scene, because the story is about Isaac wooing Rebecca, so once again there's a romantic undertone.
- Nobody can guess what word the Isaac and Rebecca scene is supposed to represent, so Rochester and Blanche act out the whole phrase. This time Rochester is dressed like a prisoner in a cell.
- The team that's guessing correctly identifies the word or phrase they're acting out as "Bridewell," which is a prison. (So the second scene represented the word "well.")
- Blanche giggles obnoxiously about the way she and Rochester just got "married."
- The teams switch, and some other people start acting out their scenes. Jane doesn't notice anything they do because she's watching Mr. Rochester.
- Rochester is letting Blanche flirt with him and kind of flirting back, but Jane can tell that he really sees through her. This makes it much worse for Jane: she can tell Rochester doesn't really love Blanche, and she can also tell that Blanche isn't worthy of him, but it seems like he's going to marry her anyway. If he were really smitten, or Blanche were a better person, Jane claims she wouldn't mind so much.
- Jane also notices that Blanche isn't very good at pleasing Rochester. The few times that Jane has been with him alone, she's figured out how to get him in a good mood, and Blanche can't do it.
- Rochester is more interesting to Jane than ever; she's come to like his rudeness and sarcastic nature, because they make him a deeper person. She also notices that, in spite of the way he behaves, Rochester is pretty much the life and soul of the party, and when he's gone everyone else seems depressed.
- One day Rochester has to go to the nearest town (Millcote) on some kind of business, and everyone's pretty bored, especially Blanche Ingram. Just before dinner, with Rochester still absent, a stranger arrives at Thornfield.
- The stranger is a polite man in his thirties or forties; he has an unusual accent and claims to be an old friend of Mr. Rochester's. He joins the group for dinner while he waits for Rochester to come back.
- Jane evaluates him and decides that he's the exact opposite of Mr. Rochester – in fact, she suggests that, if Mr. Rochester is a sheepdog, this guy is a sheep. The other women at dinner think he's adorable, which just proves that they're ninnies.
- Sitting with the group in the drawing-room (remember Rochester ordered her to join them every night), Jane learns more about the stranger: his last name is Mason, he's from the West Indies, and that's where he met Mr. Rochester.
- Suddenly, a strange gypsy woman arrives. There's a gypsy camp in the area and some of the women had wanted to visit it, but they couldn't because it rained too much that day. Now one of the gypsy women has come to them offering to tell their fortunes.
- Some of the guests want to send the woman away, but a few of the women are excited about getting their fortunes told, and the old woman refuses to leave until she tells the fortune of each and every woman there.

- Blanche Ingram insists that they let the gypsy woman tell their fortunes. The woman insists that the servants put her in a little room by herself and the guests go in to see her one by one.
- One of the men wants to check the gypsy out first to make sure it's safe for the ladies to see her, but the gypsy woman says that she'll only tell fortunes for the young, single women in the group.
- Blanche Ingram goes first. Everyone waits excitedly for her to come back and tell them what the woman said, but when she does come back she's all grumpy-pants, says the woman is obviously a fraud, and starts reading a book and ignoring everyone.
- Each of the other single women – Mary Ingram, Amy Eshton, and Louisa Eshton – goes to have her fortune told with lots of "hysterical giggling and little shrieks." They come back amazed at how much the gypsy seems to know about them.
- The servant, Sam, tells Jane that the gypsy woman says she knows there's another single woman in the group, and that he thinks that must mean her. Jane's curious about the woman, so she goes to see her and have her own fortune told.

Volume II, Chapter Four

- Jane enters the library and sees the old gypsy woman reading a prayer-book by the fire. Her hat and handkerchief throw shadows over her face.
- The woman starts telling Jane her fortune; Jane is calm and amused, and doesn't believe a word of it. When the woman describes Jane as lonely and unloved, Jane points out that almost anyone in her situation (governess at an isolated rural house) would fit that description. We're guessing Jane wouldn't believe in horoscopes, either.
- Next the woman tells Jane that she is "very near happiness" and that everything is in place for her happily-ever-after ending, but that something needs to happen first. Jane refuses to be baited, and says she can't guess the riddle.
- Jane does seem at least a little interested – she pays the woman a shilling. The woman says she can't read Jane's palm, and that reading palms doesn't work anyway, but that she can read Jane's face. Jane's much more willing to believe that you can read faces – remember all that phrenology stuff from Volume I, Chapter 14?
- The woman tries to get Jane to tell her what she's thinking and feeling. She even tries to prove that she knows Jane by describing how Jane likes to sit in the window seat, but Jane laughs at this and says that she must have learned that from the servants.
- The woman admits that she knows Grace Poole. This is getting sinister.
- Jane says that sometimes she thinks about saving up her money and starting a little school of her own, but the woman wants to talk about romance and marriage. Jane says she doesn't care about those things.
- The gypsy asks Jane about Mr. Rochester, and when she doesn't say much in response, the gypsy suggests that Mr. Rochester is in love with Blanche Ingram. Jane admits that the rumor is that Rochester and Blanche are engaged, but corrects the woman on one thing – they're not in love.
- The old woman keeps talking about Mr. Rochester, and Jane says she wants to hear her own fortune, not his.

- The gypsy asks Jane to kneel on the hearthrug and studies her face, describing its features: Jane's eyes, which are "soft and full of feeling" but show that she's laughing silently at the woman; Jane's mouth, which the woman says is meant to laugh and talk and not be so stern all the time; and her forehead, which shows her insistence on reason and ethics.
- In a moment, the woman's voice changes – the old gypsy woman is Mr. Rochester in disguise, and he's just been messing with everyone. He can't bring himself to tease Jane any more, though, and so he lets her know who he is.
- Rochester takes off his costume and asks Jane what she thinks. Jane's not sure whether she's upset. It bothers her that Rochester was trying to get her to "talk nonsense," maybe by getting her to admit that she's attracted to him, but she didn't end up saying anything embarrassing, so she thinks she can forgive him.
- Rochester asks Jane to stay and tell him what everyone else was saying about the different "fortunes" he told the women and any other news. She tells him about Mason's arrival, and he's so horrified that he can't even stand up anymore. Clearly, Mason's presence means something terrible has happened, or will happen.
- Jane helps Rochester to a chair. This is the second time he's had to lean on her shoulder. (Remember the first, in Volume I, Chapter 12?)
- Rochester tells Jane that he wishes they were alone on a deserted island together. She offers to do anything for him – even if she has to sacrifice her own life. He assures her that he'll let her know if she can help.
- Rochester sends Jane to get him a glass of wine and to see what everyone's doing in the other room. She comes back and tells him everyone is laughing and chatting as usual; he seems a little relieved.
- Rochester asks Jane what she would do if everyone else in the party rejected him; she says she wouldn't care at all. He's a little bit happier after this, and asks her to go and send Mason to see him. She does, and then goes to bed. Lying awake, she hears Mr. Rochester come upstairs with Mr. Mason, show him to a room politely, then go to his own room, and this makes her feel better.

Volume II, Chapter Five

- Jane is woken up by bright moonlight, and then startled by a strange shriek from the third floor. Then she hears thumping and banging upstairs, as though people are fighting, and calls for help. Someone is calling for Mr. Rochester.
- Everyone in the house is woken up by all the noise. The guests stumble around in the corridor in their robes, but nobody seems to know what's going on.
- Rochester tells them that a servant had a nightmare and assigns the gentlemen to make the ladies go back to bed.
- Jane goes back to her room and gets dressed, then sits by the window waiting. She knows something else is going to happen.
- After about an hour, everyone else has fallen asleep again. Jane keeps waiting, and eventually Mr. Rochester knocks on her door and asks her to come with him.
- When they get to the third floor, Rochester has an idea and sends Jane back to get a

sponge and some salts. (These are smelling salts, which have a strong, disgusting smell, and are used to wake up people who have fainted or passed out.)

- Jane comes back, and Rochester unlocks the door to the third floor – the same door Jane has seen Grace Poole go through. They enter, and Jane can hear Grace's weird laugh. Mr. Rochester goes ahead of her into the next room and gives instructions.
- Rochester comes back, and leads Jane into another part of the first room, where Mr. Mason is sitting in a chair. He's pale and passed out, and one of his arms is soaked in his own blood.
- While Jane holds the candle, Rochester wakes Mason with the smelling salts. Rochester also checks on Mason's wound; there's a bandage around Mason's arm and shoulder, but the bleeding hasn't stopped.
- Rochester tells Jane to stay with Mason and to make sure he stays awake, but not to talk to him at all for any reason. He gives her the sponge, which is bloody now, so that she can tend to the wound a little, too.
- Then Mr. Rochester leaves, locking them in the room. Jane's afraid to be locked in with a dying man when his murderess is just in the next room, but she does what she has to do.
- For a long time, maybe two hours, Jane stays there, wiping blood and gore off Mason's chest, trying to keep him conscious, and feeling utterly afraid of the woman in the next room.
- Every so often she hears weird, snarling noises, as though it were a dog and not a woman nearby. She wonders what horrible thing lives at Thornfield that Mr. Rochester can't seem to fight or destroy.
- Finally, Mr. Rochester comes back with a doctor, Mr. Carter. He gives the doctor half an hour to get Mason bandaged correctly before they take Mason away.
- While the doctor works, Mason and Rochester talk about what happened, but they don't say enough to really explain.
- The doctor notices that Mason wasn't stabbed – he was bitten.
- Rochester says that he warned Mason, and Mason should have listened. Mason says he thought he could have done something to make things better. Jane wants to know what the heck is going on, and so do we.
- Mason mentions that "she" sucked the blood from the wound after biting him – is Grace Poole a vampire?
- Rochester is worried about getting Mason out of the house before dawn. He sends Jane to fetch various pieces of clothing to get Mason and the doctor ready.
- Rochester gives Mason a few drops of a red cordial that he got in Rome; it seems to help him revive a little, and he's able to walk downstairs with the doctor holding him up.
- Together, Rochester, and the doctor help Mason get downstairs and into a carriage, while Jane acts as lookout.
- Just before Mason is driven away, he asks Rochester to take care of "her" as gently as possible.
- Rochester and Jane are left alone together outside the house, and he asks her to walk with him in the woods as the sun is rising before they go back to Thornfield Hall. They stroll, and he picks a rose for her.
- Rochester asks Jane about the last few hours, and seems worried that she felt so afraid. He tells Jane that he will be in danger until Mason leaves England.
- Jane's confused – Mason seems harmless. Rochester explains that Mason could destroy him by accidentally saying the wrong thing, and that he can't let Mason know how much

damage he could cause.

- Rochester muses on Jane's faithfulness; he can tell that Jane enjoys helping him, but also that she would never follow his orders if she thought they were morally wrong.
- Jane and Rochester sit together on a bench; this is the first time she has taken a place at his side. Rochester asks her to imagine something: she is a spoiled young man in a foreign country, and there she accidentally makes a terrible mistake with long-lasting consequences. Hmm, who do you think he's really talking about?
- Anyway, this *completely hypothetical* young man tries to get past these consequences, and travels all around the world amusing himself with superficial pleasures. After twenty years, he meets a new friend and feels completely regenerated and changed. Hmm, who might this "friend" be? Rochester's pretty obvious about things.
- So, anyway, the "hypothetical" man now wants to spend the rest of his life with his "friend," but he needs to break some kind of rule to do so. Rochester's question to Jane is: is it OK if he does?
- Jane *reeeeeally* wants to say yes, but she can tell Rochester's trying to get away with something that isn't right, even though she's not 100% sure what the problem is. She tells him that nobody should let their redemption depend on their relationship with someone else. To put it another way, this hypothetical guy has to sort out his problem first, and then he can be with his, erm, "friend."
- After hearing her response, Rochester gets rude and sarcastic, starts telling Jane how great Blanche Ingram is, and sends her back to the house through the woods while he goes another way to talk to Dent and Lynn, who have come out to the stables.

Volume II, Chapter Six

- Jane tells the reader about the different strange moments in her life where she and people she knew seemed to be a little bit psychic – to have premonitions, or to sense what's going on with their distant friends and family.
- Lately, Jane's been having strange nightmares about a baby. Every night for a week, she's played with this weird baby in her dreams, and it is totally creeping her out.
- One afternoon, Jane is visited by Robert Leaven, Mr. Reed's coachman, who married Jane's nursemaid Bessie. (Remember how we learned that in Volume I, Chapter 10?)
- Robert tells Jane that John Reed is dead, possibly by suicide because of his gambling debts, and that Mrs. Reed had a stroke when she heard. On her deathbed, Mrs. Reed has been asking to see Jane.
- Jane goes to ask Mr. Rochester for time off work (after all, she's still Adèle's governess) so that she can visit Mrs. Reed. Rochester makes her explain everything about the situation, and at first refuses to let Jane go a hundred miles away to see someone who was so cruel to her.
- Eventually Jane persuades Rochester to let her go, although she can't promise when she'll be back.
- Rochester realizes Jane will need some money so that she can travel safely; he hasn't paid her yet for any of her work as a governess. He's not cheating her; it's just that there's no need for Jane to have money while living at Thornfield, so he hasn't bothered.

- Jane only has five shillings total in the whole world, so Rochester offers her fifty pounds. It's tough to say exactly what that means in hard cash today, but remember that Jane's annual salary is thirty pounds *a year*, and she's only worked six months so far, so he only owes her fifteen, and he's being far too generous, basically paying her three times what he owes.
- Jane won't take more than she's earned, and Rochester ends up giving her ten pounds because he doesn't have exact change for fifteen. He tells her maybe it will help that he owes her five more – it will make her come back.
- While they're doing business, Jane tells Rochester that she's going to advertise for a new governess job, because she knows that after he marries Blanche they will send Adèle to school.
- Rochester's pretty upset about the possibility of losing Jane, and teases her by trying to make her give back the ten pounds.
- When Jane refuses to give back her salary, Rochester makes her promise that she won't place an ad applying for other jobs. She agrees, but makes him promise that she and Adèle will both be out of Thornfield before he marries Blanche.
- Jane and Rochester say goodbye; Rochester seems to want to say more, but doesn't.
- The next morning, Jane leaves for Gateshead very early, and arrives at the lodge a few days later at five in the afternoon. Bessie and Robert are there with their children, and Jane has tea with them. Lots of old memories of Bessie as a nursemaid come flooding back to Jane. Jane tells Bessie all about Mr. Rochester and Thornfield.
- After tea, Bessie and Jane walk to the main house. This is the first time Jane's been back since she left for Lowood nine years ago.
- When Jane enters the house, everything looks just the same, except for the people. She sees Eliza and Georgiana Reed. Eliza is super-uptight, dressed all in black with her hair pulled back tight and a sour expression. Georgiana is plump, blonde, and blue-eyed, also dressed in black because they're mourning their brother's death, but much more fashionable.
- Eliza and Georgiana chat snobbily with Jane for a little bit, making it clear that they think she's definitely their inferior. Jane, however, is all grown up now, and she doesn't care what they do or say.
- Jane asks her cousins about Mrs. Reed, and they seem offended to be asked a direct question and uninterested in arranging Jane's visit. Jane ignores them and arranges her own visit, deciding to stay until Mrs. Reed is better or until she has died.
- Jane goes in to see Mrs. Reed, who is, of course, lying ill in bed. Jane's interested to realize that she doesn't feel bitter toward Mrs. Reed anymore – just sorry for her and willing to forgive her.
- Mrs. Reed is still harsh and bad-tempered, but she does want Jane to stay so that they can talk things over. Unfortunately, Mrs. Reed is also losing her mind a little – sometimes she starts talking to Jane about Jane as though she were someone else.
- While Mrs. Reed is raving, Jane gets her to explain why she always hated her niece. Apparently, Jane's mother was Mr. Reed's sister, and when the family disowned her for marrying a man of low status, Mr. Reed defended her. Mr. Reed was always attached to his sister and her child, Jane Eyre, and Mrs. Reed seems to have been jealous.
- It becomes clear that Mrs. Reed doesn't really know that her son has committed suicide – she's still worried about his money problems and his threats to kill himself or her.
- Mrs. Reed falls into a sort of coma, and Jane doesn't get a chance to talk to her for ten

days. In the meantime, Eliza sews and reads, Georgiana talks to the canary, and Jane sketches pictures of landscapes and fairies and elves.

- One day, Jane sketches a portrait of Mr. Rochester. She's so absorbed in staring at it that she doesn't notice her cousins come up and take a look. They're surprised that she's such a good artist and she ends up sketching their portraits.
- Jane's sketches seem to have broken the ice; Georgiana, in particular, starts to talk to Jane more and more. Unfortunately, Georgiana is completely superficial; she only talks about herself and her romances and her own problems, and never even mentions her mother's illness or her brother's suicide or anything else.
- Eliza doesn't really hang out with Jane, but it's not that she hates Jane; she's just kind of a loner. She has super-organized days where she does particular tasks – read a prayer book, work in the garden, sew – at specific times, and that's pretty much all she wants. She says that she's planning to retire to somewhere like a nunnery after her mother dies.
- Eliza and Georgiana don't really get along; sometimes Eliza lectures Georgiana about how vain and superficial she is and tells her to make herself a schedule of activities so that she can be independent and not need company. Georgiana thinks, maybe correctly, that Eliza is just jealous of her looks and romances. Eliza makes it clear that she won't have anything to do with Georgiana after their mother dies.
- One day, Eliza is at church and Georgiana has fallen asleep on the sofa, and Jane goes up to check on Mrs. Reed. Jane remembers Helen Burns' death and thinks about the afterlife.
- Mrs. Reed speaks for the first time in days. She doesn't believe who Jane is at first, but is slowly convinced.
- As she's dying, Mrs. Reed apologizes to Jane for two things: first, for not treating her like a daughter, which is what she promised Mr. Reed she would do; second, for concealing a letter from Jane's uncle, John Eyre, that came three years ago.
- Mrs. Reed lets Jane read the letter, in which John asked where Jane was so that he could write a will making her the heir of his fortune when he died. Mrs. Reed didn't tell Jane about it because she held a grudge against Jane for being ungrateful to her.
- Then Mrs. Reed admits something else: she wrote to John Eyre and told him Jane died of typhus during the epidemic at Lowood.
- Jane forgives Mrs. Reed and asks Mrs. Reed to forgive her in return, but Mrs. Reed refuses to kiss her cheek.
- Mrs. Reed loses consciousness again; Bessie and a nurse come in and take care of her, and Jane stays with them, but Mrs. Reed dies that evening without saying anything else. Neither Jane nor Eliza cries.

Volume II, Chapter Seven

- Jane stays at Gateshead for several weeks after Mrs. Reed dies, first to keep Georgiana company until she goes back to London, then to take care of the house while Eliza gets ready to move to a nunnery in France. (There are no nunneries in England at this point because it's not a Catholic country – read more on this in our Shmoop module "The Protestant Reformation," coming soon.)

- While traveling back to Thornfield, Jane realizes that she's never felt happy to go back to a place that has been her home – returning to Lowood or to Gateshead wasn't much fun.
- She wonders if returning to Thornfield might be nicer, but she's not sure how long she'll live there if Mr. Rochester is marrying Blanche Ingram. Still, at least she'll get to see the man she loves for a few weeks. She knows he won't be there when she arrives; Mrs. Fairfax told her in a letter that he had gone to London to get things for his wedding.
- Jane walks the last few miles to Thornfield, and, coming around a corner, sees Mr. Rochester sitting on a stile (a set of steps you use to climb over a fence) writing in a book. She freezes and trembles, and then he sees her and calls her over to him.
- Rochester scolds Jane for staying away from him for so long and accuses her of forgetting him. Then he tells her about the carriage he bought for the soon-to-be Mrs. Rochester, and asks if she can't use her fairy magic to make him handsome. Jane insists that his ugliness is impossible to cure, but the way she's looking at him suggests otherwise.
- Rochester moves a little and lets her cross over the stile, and before she keeps going she thanks him for his kindness and tells him that wherever he is, that's her true home. Then she walks away really fast before he can answer her.
- When Jane arrives at Thornfield, everyone is glad to see her. After dinner, Mr. Rochester, Jane, Mrs. Fairfax, and Adèle almost seem like a family.
- Interestingly, Blanche Ingram isn't around anymore; Rochester doesn't visit her, she doesn't visit him, and nobody's talking about marriage. Jane secretly hopes that the engagement is off.

Volume II, Chapter Eight

- Summer at Thornfield is incredibly beautiful this year, with bright sunlight and incredible colors in the wood and fields. Adèle gathers wild strawberries, Jane strolls in the garden, and everything seems perfect...a little TOO perfect.
- While strolling in the woods, Jane smells Rochester's cigar. She tries to sneak away from him, but he notices her at the moment that their shadows cross. Creepy.
- Rochester asks Jane to walk with him, and she can't think up an excuse not to. As they walk, he asks if she's become attached to Thornfield and its residents, and she admits that she has. He tells her that she'll have to leave soon and that he's marrying Blanche Ingram. He reminds Jane that it was her idea that, if he married Blanche, Adèle should go to school and Jane should get a new job.
- However, Mr. Rochester tells Jane not to advertise for a new position as a governess; he says he'll find a position for her himself. He has one in mind, he says, in Ireland.
- Jane is so upset at the idea of being in Ireland, far away from Thornfield and Mr. Rochester, that she starts crying. Rochester soothes her a little and says that, since they've been such good friends, they should spend a little time together before she has to leave in a few weeks.
- Jane and Rochester sit on the bench under the chestnut tree. Rochester describes his attachment to Jane; he feels, he says, as if there is a cord tied to each of their hearts that connects them, and he's worried that if she goes too far away it will snap. Jane can't say very much to this, because she's sobbing.

- Notice that there's a nightingale singing in the background; nightingales are usually Significant with a capital S. (See Shmoop's coverage of Keats' "Ode to a Nightingale," coming soon, and this article on Philomela.)
- Jane finally stops crying long enough to explain what she loves about Thornfield – mostly, her intellectual and spiritual connection with Mr. Rochester. Needing to leave him, she says, feels like death.
- The conversation gets confused; Rochester asks Jane why she has to leave, and she says that it's because of his bride, Blanche Ingram. Rochester says he doesn't have a bride; Jane says he will. Rochester says, yes, he WILL, and Jane is going to stay.
- Jane can't take this; she's hurt and angry, and she lectures Rochester on how cruel it would be to make her stay in the house and watch his marriage to someone else. Even though he's a gentleman of property and she's a governess, she still *feels* like he does – they're equal in that way.
- Rochester says they are indeed equal – and kisses her.
- Jane struggles and insists that she's going to leave him and go to Ireland.
- Rochester asks her to marry him.
- Jane thinks he's making fun of her.
- Rochester asks her to sit back down. They listen to that Significant Nightingale and try to calm down.
- After a bit of wrangling, Rochester convinces Jane that she's the only woman he wants to marry, and that he never cared about Blanche Ingram. Jane scrutinizes his face before deciding she believes him – remember how important faces were in Volume I, Chapter Fourteen and Volume II, Chapter Four? Yep, they're still important here.
- Jane and Rochester embrace...and Rochester asks God to pardon him. For what, we wonder?
- They sit on the bench together for a long time, but the night is dark and a thunderstorm begins. They hurry back into the house before they get too wet in the rain; once they're inside, Rochester kisses Jane good night...a few times. They don't notice at first that Mrs. Fairfax is watching them.
- Everyone goes to bed, separately, of course. Mr. Rochester knocks on Jane's bedroom door several times in the night to ask if she's OK – the storm is raging crazily outside. Jane is fine, but, BAD OMEN ALERT, the chestnut tree gets splintered in half by lightning.

Volume II, Chapter Nine

- The next morning, Jane is blissfully happy and wonders if this is all a dream. She gives away all the money she has (a few shillings) to some beggars so they can share in her happiness.
- At breakfast, Jane feels a little uncomfortable because Rochester hasn't explained their engagement to Mrs. Fairfax yet, and Mrs. Fairfax seems a bit sad and upset about what she saw the night before, but Jane knows she'll just have to wait for Rochester to tell the housekeeper what's going on.
- When Jane goes to the school-room to teach Adèle, she discovers that Rochester has sent Adèle to the nursery and met her in the school-room himself.

- They embrace, and Rochester tells Jane that they will get married in four weeks. He calls her "Jane Rochester" and "Mrs. Rochester," teasing her a little with what will be her new name.
- Next, Rochester starts telling Jane about all the fancy jewelry and clothes he's going to give her – he plans to deck her out in the best there is and make everyone think she's beautiful. This makes Jane very uncomfortable and she tells him not to flatter her, but he keeps going.
- Rochester is also planning an elaborate honeymoon in Europe – Paris, Rome, Naples, Florence, Vienna, and more. Jane's excited at the prospect of traveling, especially together with the man she loves, but she insists that he shouldn't think of her as an angel.
- Jane presses Rochester to think about his own inconsistencies; she reminds him that he's capricious, which means his mood and behavior change frequently, and that she knows he won't be constant in the way he loves her.
- Rochester insists that he will be constant in his love for Jane, because she's different from all the other women he's known. She behaves submissively, but in doing so she actually masters him. Does that sound familiar? Jane thinks it sounds like the legend of Hercules or the story of Samson; we think it sounds a bit like *The Taming of the Shrew*...with Rochester as the shrew!
- Rochester tells Jane that she has only to ask, and he'll do any favor she wants. She asks him to answer a question. He seems very nervous at first about what it might be, but then she asks why he made her think he was going to marry Blanche Ingram, and he seems relieved.
- Rochester explains that he pretended to be interested in Blanche so that Jane would be jealous and fall more in love with him – he was already in love with her (Jane).
- Jane asks about Blanche's feelings, and Rochester says her only feeling is pride, and that needs to be trampled on. He reminds Jane that he circulated a rumor that his fortune was actually very small, and then Blanche and her mother stopped being interested in him – so they're just gold-diggers anyway.
- Jane asks Rochester for another favor: tell Mrs. Fairfax about their engagement. Rochester sends Jane upstairs to put on her bonnet so they can go into town, and while she's gone he talks to Mrs. Fairfax.
- Jane comes back downstairs, and, when she hears Mr. Rochester leave Mrs. Fairfax's room, she goes in. Mrs. Fairfax is shocked; she's not upset, exactly, but really confused about why someone like Rochester – wealthy and nearly forty – would be interested in Jane – who is poor, plain, and young. Mrs. Fairfax cautions Jane about some of the problems that might turn up in her relationship with Rochester, but Jane is insulted by her suggestions.
- Adèle interrupts and insists on going with Jane and Rochester in the carriage. At first Rochester refuses, because he wants to be alone with Jane, but when he sees how upset she is that he's still ordering her around, he agrees.
- Adèle asks questions about what will happen now that Jane and Rochester are going to get married; Rochester says that Adèle will go to school on her own, and he and Jane will fly to the moon and live in a cave together, alone.
- Adèle doesn't believe Rochester's silly claims about living on the moon, eating manna, and wearing clouds and rainbows, so he tells her a story instead. The "story" is his version of the moment when Jane found him sitting on the stile writing – and in his version, Jane is a fairy, who offers him a golden ring that can make him fly to another world.

- Adèle's too old for these fairy stories, and laughs at Rochester.
- In Millcote, Rochester wants to buy Jane six new gowns in bright colors to replace her plain Lowood-style wardrobe of grey and black. Jane manages to argue him down to two new gowns, black satin and grey silk. Then Rochester starts buying her fancy jewelry, but Jane feels degraded.
- Suddenly, Jane remembers her uncle, John Eyre, who wanted to leave her his fortune. Even if it's not very much, Jane thinks it would be nice to have a little financial independence; that way Rochester can't dress her like a doll all the time. She regains her composure, looks him in the eye, and tells him that, if he keeps decking her out in expensive clothes and jewelry and behaving so badly about it, she'll never wear anything he buys her.
- Rochester laughs, and says that Jane is better than a whole harem. Jane tells him that, if he wants a harem, he should go east and start buying slave girls, because she's certainly not going to be one for him. Rochester asks what she would do if he did, and she says she'd become a missionary and go and preach to his slaves and ferment a rebellion. They're teasing each other, but something serious is going on here, too.
- Rochester asks what terms Jane wants in their relationship, and she tells him that she's not going to be like his previous mistress, Céline Varens – a kept woman, who is given lots of expensive presents by her lover. She wants to keep being Adèle's governess, earning her wages, and not getting any extra presents until she is actually Rochester's wife. She even refuses to have dinner with him – as governess, she never had dinner with the master before, and she won't start now.
- Rochester tells Jane that she can make her terms now, but once they're married, he'll run the show. Again, he's teasing...but he's also serious.
- Jane knows how to manage Rochester. They arrive home in the carriage, and Jane puts Adèle to bed. They dine separately, as they have done in the past, and then Rochester sends for Jane after dinner. But Jane's got a plan to keep him occupied and prevent him from behaving seductively.
- Jane teases Rochester into playing the piano and singing a song. At first he doesn't want to, but when she plays and sings herself, he can't help but push her aside and do better.
- Rochester sings a love song that pretty much summarizes his relationship with Jane; at the end of it, they're both feeling pretty lovey-dovey, but Jane forces herself to keep teasing him and keeping him at a distance; she doesn't want another inappropriate show of affection, like when Mr. Rochester kissed her in the hallway in front of Mrs. Fairfax.
- When Rochester tries to get Jane to be all sentimental with him, she argues with him and makes him angry and irritated instead. She'd rather they were verbally sparring than being nauseatingly mushy.
- Jane can tell that this is the right approach for Rochester – if she let him make their relationship into a smoochy Hallmark cuddle-fest, he'd get bored with it really fast, and so would she.
- Jane also notices that Mrs. Fairfax approves her keeping Rochester at arm's length.
- It's difficult for Jane to keep this up, though, because she's falling so deeply in love with him – even idolizing him and putting him between herself and God. Uh-oh.

Volume II, Chapter Ten

- The four weeks are almost over, and now it's the night before Jane and Rochester's wedding. Jane is looking at the name and address on her honeymoon luggage, and she can't believe in this new "Jane Rochester" person just yet.
- Jane goes outside for an evening walk; she's upset about something she saw the night before, and she's waiting for Rochester to come home so she can tell him about it.
- SYMBOLISM ALERT: The wind is blowing wildly outside, and Jane runs through it to look at the splintered chestnut tree. (Remember that it was struck by lightning at the end of Volume II, Chapter Eight.) Jane tells the tree – yes, she's talking to a tree, folks – that it was right for the two halves to cling together, even though they're dying and the tree won't live much longer. Hmm, who might the two halves of the tree represent?
- Jane starts doing chores to keep herself busy while waiting for Rochester. She gathers the windfall apples off the ground in the orchard, sorts them, and brings them into the storeroom. She makes sure there's a fire in Rochester's study.
- She still can't sit still waiting for him, so she runs down to the gate to meet him there. She can't wait patiently, and she starts walking along the road toward the town, hoping to meet him halfway.
- After about a quarter-mile, Jane meets Rochester on the road. He helps her up onto his horse and they keep riding toward Thornfield. Jane is soaked (it's raining) and a bit feverish, and Rochester's worried that she's been upset about something.
- They reach Thornfield; Jane changes out of her wet clothes, and Rochester eats dinner. Jane sits with Rochester, but won't eat with him, and then they sit together talking, even though it's midnight. Jane keeps telling Rochester that her whole life seems like a dream right now, and he's the most unreal part of it.
- Rochester tries to get Jane to explain what she's upset about; she's not nervous about what kind of husband he'll be, or about becoming a "lady," or anything else you might expect. She's upset about the weird thing that happened last night, and so she tells Rochester the story:
- The previous evening, Jane was happy and busy, and spent some time walking in the garden just before sunset, feeling grateful that everything was going so well in her life.
- At sunset, she went inside, and found that Rochester had sent a package from London with an expensive wedding veil for her to wear. She decided that she would wear the much simpler one she had prepared anyway, and that she would tease him about trying to deck her out in stuff that's too fancy for her.
- Jane went to bed, but couldn't sleep. She thought she could hear a weird howling sound in the wind.
- Jane fell asleep and started dreaming, but in her dream she missed Rochester and felt separated from him – not just because they were a long distance apart, but in some other, strange way.
- Jane dreamed that she was walking along a road carrying a small child, and Rochester was somewhere ahead of her on the road, but she couldn't catch up with him because she had to carry the child.
- Rochester comforts Jane, saying that the dream was just a dream, but their love for one another is real. Jane affirms that she loves him completely, and for some reason this makes him sad. He asks her to tease him instead of being so sincere.

- Jane tells Rochester that her story isn't finished, and continues:
- Next, Jane dreamed that Thornfield hall was a ruin, and she was walking around in the ruin carrying the same child. She heard a horse and knew that Mr. Rochester was riding up to the house, and she climbed a wall to get a glimpse of him, but the wall crumbled and she fell and dropped the child. Then she woke up.
- When Jane woke up, there was a burning candle on the table in her room. She thought that maybe Adèle's nursemaid Sophie was in the room and called her name.
- Then Jane noticed that her closet door was open and someone was messing with her wedding dress and veil. Someone came out of the closet, took the candle, and used the light from the candle to examine Jane's trousseau and honeymoon luggage.
- Jane sat up in bed, shocked: the woman wasn't anyone she knew at Thornfield, but someone else, a stranger.
- The stranger was a tall woman with long, dark hair dressed in white; her face was disturbing, with bloodshot red eyes, swollen, dark lips, and thick black eye-brows. It looked like a vampire!
- SYMBOLISM ALERT: The strange woman was wearing Jane's wedding veil, and, as Jane watched, the woman pulled it off, tore it in half, and trampled on it.
- The figure leaned close to Jane, who was sitting up in bed, held the candle close to her face, and then snuffed it. Jane fainted. (Remember that Jane has only fainted from fear once before – see Volume I, Chapter 2.)
- Jane woke up in her room alone in the morning and decided not to tell anyone what happened except for Mr. Rochester.
- Jane asks Mr. Rochester who the woman is. Rochester says that she imagined this nightmarish creature, and Jane insists that it all really happened.
- Rochester tries to convince her that the appearance of the strange woman was just one more dream – but it can't have been a dream, because Jane found her wedding veil on the floor in two pieces. Rochester is glad she wasn't harmed.
- Next, Rochester tells Jane that it must have been Grace Poole who did this, even though Jane said earlier that it definitely wasn't Grace. He says that Jane imagined the woman as looking like a vampire or goblin because she was half-dreaming.
- Jane's not really satisfied with this explanation, but she pretends to be to make Rochester feel better.
- Rochester insists that Jane sleep in Adèle's bed tonight so that she will have Sophie and Adèle for company. Jane obeys him and tells him she's calm, but she doesn't sleep a wink. She lies awake a night holding the sleeping Adèle in her arms and waiting.
- In the morning, Jane has to pull Adèle off of her so that she can leave. She cries and cries as she puts Adèle down and leaves the room; she feels like Adèle represents her past, and now she's going out to meet the future without knowing what's going to happen.

Volume II, Chapter Eleven

- In the morning, Sophie dresses Jane in her wedding gown and plain veil (since the fancy veil was destroyed by the mysterious vampire-like woman in the previous chapter).
- Mr. Rochester is impatient to get to the church and then to start off for London for the

beginning of the honeymoon.

- The church is just past the gate of Thornfield, so Rochester and Jane walk the short way there. They have no attendants, family, or friends there for the wedding – just the usual servants.
- Rochester is practically marching Jane to the church, holding her arm in an iron grasp. As they arrive in the churchyard, he realizes he's being cruel to her, and lets her catch her breath.
- While they're waiting in the churchyard, Jane notices two men, strangers. They slip around the corner of the church. Mr. Rochester doesn't see them.
- Jane and Rochester enter the church; the priest is there waiting, and so are the two strangers. The wedding ceremony begins.
- When the priest gets to the part where he asks if anyone knows any reason why the bride and groom "may not lawfully be joined together in matrimony" – you know, the "speak now, or forever hold your peace" bit – one of the strangers comes forward and says he does know a reason.
- Rochester stands frozen and rigid, refusing to turn and look at the stranger.
- The reason that Rochester can't marry Jane, according to the stranger, is that *Rochester is already married to someone else.*
- Jane looks to Rochester, but all he does is hold her close to him and ask the stranger to describe his supposed wife.
- The stranger, a lawyer named Mr. Briggs, reads a statement from Richard Mason, which claims that, fifteen years before, Rochester married a woman named Bertha Mason in Jamaica, and that he has a copy of the marriage certificate to prove it.
- Rochester says that the statement proves he was once married, but not that his wife is alive today.
- Briggs says that he has a witness who saw Bertha alive three months before. The second stranger comes forward – and it's Richard Mason.
- Rochester is completely pissed, so furious that the priest has to remind him he's in church before he does something to Mason.
- Mason says that he is Bertha's brother and that he saw her at Thornfield hall in April (it's now just after mid-summer, sometime in late June).
- The priest, Mr. Wood, says that he has lived in the area for a long time and never heard of a Mrs. Rochester at Thornfield. Mr. Rochester says he made sure nobody would hear about her.
- Somewhat angrily, Rochester explains that he was, in fact, trying to commit bigamy, and that he realizes how sinful and immoral this makes him.
- Rochester reminds Wood, and everyone else there, that they may not have heard of a Mrs. Rochester, but they probably have heard that there's a strange lunatic kept at Thornfield Hall. Some of the rumors are that the lunatic is his half-sister; other people say she's his former mistress; but now he admits that she is his wife, Bertha Mason.
- Bertha, according to Rochester, is insane; madness runs in her family, and he was tricked into marrying her before he realized that she had inherited it. He invites everyone in the church to come back to Thornfield and see just what his "wife" is like.
- Rochester also emphasizes to them that Jane didn't know about Rochester's previous marriage and thought that the wedding was completely legal.
- Rochester, Jane, Mr. Wood, Mr. Briggs, and Mr. Mason walk back to Thornfield. Rochester sends away the carriage, because they won't need it – there isn't going to be any

honeymoon.

- Rochester takes everyone up to the third floor and unlocks the door of the room where Mason was bitten and stabbed.
- They go through a second door into the next room and find Grace Poole cooking something over the fire and Bertha on the other side of the room, moving on all fours, growling and behaving like a wild animal.
- Rochester asks Grace how her patient is doing, and Grace says that she's alright today – but when Bertha sees Rochester, she goes crazy. Rochester protects Jane by coming between her and Bertha, and Bertha attacks Rochester, trying to bite his cheek.
- Rochester and Bertha struggle until he gets her arms behind her back, and Grace Poole helps him tie her to a chair.
- Rochester asks everyone to consider the kind of "marriage" he's likely to have with Bertha and to compare her to Jane. Then he throws everyone out of the room except himself, Grace and Bertha, and stays behind to give some instructions.
- As Jane and the others leave, Mr. Briggs tells her that he and Mr. Mason know her uncle, Mr. John Eyre, who is currently living in Madeira. Mason and John Eyre were friends, and when Jane wrote a letter to her uncle telling him that she was going to marry Mr. Rochester, Mason heard about it and came back to England to prevent Rochester from committing bigamy.
- Mr. Briggs tells Jane that her uncle is dying, but that he will probably die before she could reach him if she went to Madeira to see him.
- Mr. Briggs, Mr. Mason, and Mr. Wood leave, and Jane locks herself in her room. She takes off the wedding dress and puts on one of her regular, plain dresses. Then she starts to try and think about what's just happened.
- All Jane's hopes have been crushed, and, although she still loves Mr. Rochester, she doesn't trust him in the same way. She knows she has to leave Thornfield.
- Jane thinks of a prayer, but can't seem to say the words, and she feels hit by a flood of anguish and depression. Cheery, eh?

Volume III, Chapter One

- Jane stays in her room for most of the day with a debate raging in her head: Does she really have to leave Thornfield?
- When Jane finally emerges from her room, Rochester is waiting for her outside. She is faint and dizzy, and Rochester carries her downstairs to a sofa in the library and gives her a glass of wine.
- Jane won't let Rochester embrace her, although she doesn't say much.
- Rochester guesses that Jane is planning to remain at Thornfield as Adèle's governess, but cut off their intimate relationship. He proposes an alternate plan: he'll send Adèle to school, and he and Jane will go off somewhere else together.
- At this point, Rochester explains a little more about his behavior toward Bertha. He ordered the servants to keep Bertha a secret from the governess because the thought no governess would stay at Thornfield if she knew there was a madwoman there.
- Rochester says that he could have sent Bertha to another house he owns, Ferndean

Manor, but he was afraid that it was too damp and unhealthy there and that it would kill her. Hmm, remember how the problem with Lowood was that it was built in a damp, unhealthy spot that caused an epidemic of typhus? (See Book I, Chapter Nine.)

- Rochester thinks aloud, making plans to leave Thornfield and Bertha in the care of Mrs. Poole and her son. Jane rebukes him for being so cruel in his attitude toward Bertha; after all, she can't help being crazy.
- Rochester tells Jane that he doesn't hate Bertha because she's mad, and claims that, if Jane were mad, he would still take tender care of her and never abandon her to other people.
- Anyway, Rochester says he'll leave tomorrow. Jane refuses to go with him, but also realizes that he's half-wild and about to get violent, so she coaxes him into sitting down with her to talk it through.
- Jane hasn't cried yet, but now she lets herself weep and weep. She hopes that it will irritate Rochester and keep him from being so absorbed in his own sadness. It works.
- After they're both calm, Rochester asks Jane if she's upset because she just wanted his fortune and rank, instead of his love. Jane's insulted – of course she loves him, but they can't indulge in that anymore.
- Jane breaks it to Rochester that she has to leave him – permanently.
- Rochester wants Jane to go with him to France and live with him in a villa there as his "virtual" wife. He claims that he's not really married and that Jane would basically be his wife, not his mistress.
- Jane refuses this arrangement, and tells him that, with his wife alive, she would be his mistress if they ran off to France together, and saying anything else is just a lie.
- Rochester decides that Jane might change her mind if she knew the circumstances under which he married Bertha, so he tells the story:
- Edward Rochester's father didn't want to divide his fortune, so he left it all to his eldest son, Rowland, but he wanted Edward to be wealthy, too. He found the rich Mason family in Jamaica and arranged for Edward to marry Bertha Mason.
- Edward only saw Bertha at parties and for brief moments, and she was beautiful and could play the piano, sing, and so on. Everyone encouraged him, and she seemed to be great, so he married her, the way the two families wanted.
- After his marriage, Rochester found out that Bertha's mother was in an insane asylum and that her two brothers had mental problems, too.
- Rochester lived with Bertha in Jamaica for four years, even though she was hot-tempered, violent, and coarse. She was also "intemperate and unchaste" – a drunk and promiscuous.
- Rochester's father and brother died, and Rochester inherited the family fortune and lands.
- Rochester wanted to divorce Bertha for her behavior, but he couldn't because she had been diagnosed as insane.
- One evening, in stormy, hot weather, Rochester was woken by Bertha's curses and profanity and decided that he couldn't live this way anymore.
- Rochester considered suicide, but decided to go back to Europe, lock Bertha up at Thornfield, and travel on the continent. Nobody in England knew about his marriage in Jamaica.
- Rochester also decided that he wouldn't recognize Bertha as his wife anymore and that his only responsibility toward her was to make sure that she was cared for properly.
- Rochester did all this, and only Grace Poole, who has taken care of Bertha at Thornfield, and the doctor, Mr. Carter, knew about Bertha – not even Mrs. Fairfax knew, although she

might have suspected.

- Bertha has been secretive and cunning, and whenever Grace Poole turned her back, she got into mischief – most recently, of course, by trying to burn Rochester alive in his bed, stabbing her brother, and tearing Jane's wedding veil.
- After Rochester found Grace to take care of Bertha, he went to the European continent and traveled, lookin' for love in all the wrong places. He was planning to get married again, without telling the new wife or anyone else that, legally, he was committing bigamy.
- Rochester bummed around Europe for ten years. OK, he's rich, so it wasn't exactly bumming, but you get the idea. He looked for the right girl everywhere, but couldn't find anyone. He got depressed and drank a lot.
- Eventually Rochester tried having mistresses, since he couldn't find anyone he wanted to marry. He had three – Céline Varens, Giacinta, and Clara (French, Italian, and German), but none of them suited him for long.
- Rochester interrupts his own story to notice that Jane disapproves of his having mistresses. He says that he regrets it and wouldn't do it again, because it made him feel like he was buying slaves. Then he finishes the story:
- Last January, after getting rid of the last mistress, Rochester came back to England, grumpy and depressed. The first person he met, before he even got back to Thornfield, was Jane (see Book I, Chapter 12.)
- Rochester was immediately attracted to Jane and glad to find out that she was the new governess and therefore living at his house.
- The next day Rochester secretly spied on Jane while she was teaching Adèle and when she was alone, and he liked what he saw.
- Rochester was first interested in what kind of person Jane was, because she was different from everyone else he had known, and then gradually became fond of her.
- Jane interrupts Rochester and asks him not to talk about the past and how they fell in love anymore. Rochester asks her if she understands, now, that he doesn't really have a wife, despite being married to Bertha. He asks Jane to promise to be his – but she won't.
- Rochester tries his best persuasions – being sweet, being seductive, and pleading – but Jane won't do something that she thinks is wrong.
- Next Rochester reminds Jane that the only thing she'll be doing wrong if she agrees to stay with him is to break a social rule – she doesn't have any family who would be upset or harmed by her choice.
- Jane realizes that what matters most is her own respect for herself, and that it's even more important for her to cling to her principles at this difficult moment.
- Rochester is furious, and he grasps Jane tightly in his arms. He's frustrated by the fact that he could overpower her physically, but he could never capture the part of her that he's most interested in.
- Despite Rochester's pleadings, Jane leaves, giving him a kiss on the cheek and a blessing as she goes.
- That night, Jane dreams about being in the red-room at Gateshead and seeing the spirit of the moon come to her and warn her to "flee temptation."
- Jane wakes up early and packs a few small things, leaving all the presents Rochester bought her. She sneaks out of the house, pausing outside Rochester's door, tempted to relent and go to him – but she forces herself to leave. She takes a little bread and water from the kitchen as she goes.
- Jane walks along the road in the opposite direction to the local town, Millcote. She goes

until she faints down on the ground, crawls for awhile, then gets back up and walks some more. Eventually a coach comes along that's on its way to a place Jane's never heard of, and she pays the last of her money to get on it.

Volume III, Chapter Two

- Two days later, the coachman leaves Jane somewhere called Whitcross because her money has run out. Whitcross is just a crossroads, not a town, so she has at least ten miles to walk, but it's getting dark so she can't start now.
- Jane walks out into the heath and finds a place on the moor to sleep while she thinks about what to do and where to go.
- Jane feels like she's being taken care of by Mother Nature; she finds a dry, warm place to sleep and even some berries to eat.
- Jane can't sleep because she's so worried about Mr. Rochester and has to pray for him before she can fall asleep.
- In the morning, Jane wakes up early, goes back to Whitcross, and starts walking down one of the roads pretty much at random. After several hours she hears a church bell, which leads her to a small village.
- Jane sees a little bakery in the village; she's out of money, but she thinks maybe she can trade a silk handkerchief or gloves for food. When she goes into the shop, she's too ashamed to try bartering, and just asks for a place to sit down.
- Jane questions the woman working at the store about job opportunities for women in the area, but there isn't really anything available that she could do.
- Jane stays in the little town, wandering around, for over an hour, but can't think of any reason to ask to go into any of the houses. Eventually she goes up to the door of a nice-looking house and asks if they need a servant, but they don't. They're nice to her, but can't help her.
- Although she wants to slink away and rest in the forest, Jane knows she won't be able to rest while she's so hungry.
- Eventually Jane decides that the best thing to do would be to go to the parsonage and ask the local clergyman for help and advice. She goes back to the church, finds the parsonage beside it, and asks for the clergyman, but he's out of town.
- Jane goes back to the bakery and offers to trade her handkerchief or gloves for a roll or even half of a little cake, but the woman won't barter with her.
- Jane keeps walking. That evening, she passes a farmhouse, where she sees a farmer eating bread and cheese. She asks him for a piece of bread, which he gives to her without saying anything.
- Jane sleeps in the wood, but she has to keep moving so that nobody finds her, and at one point it rains. She's soaked.
- The next day, Jane keeps wandering around and asking around for work, but can't find any. In the evening, she gets a little more food – a bowl of old, sticky, congealed porridge that a girl was going to feed to a pig.
- Jane finally turns away from the village (she's already on the outskirts of it anyway) and walks toward a hill. She looks for a little hollow in the side of the hill where she can curl up

and sleep, but instead she sees a light shining in the distance. She's pretty much given up hope of finding help anywhere, but she goes toward the light anyway.

- When Jane reaches the light, she discovers that it comes from a large-ish house. Through one window, Jane sees a nice, clean room with some expensive furniture and a fire burning. There's an old woman in the room knitting, and two young ladies sitting together reading.
- As Jane watches and listens, she figures out that the two young women are actually using dictionaries to help them read and translate books that are in German. Jane learns that the old woman is a servant named Hannah and the ladies are Diana and Mary, and that the ladies are waiting for their brother St. John to come home.
- Jane also notices that the ladies are in mourning – they're wearing black, Hannah talks about missing someone who is "in a better place," and eventually one of them mentions that it was their father who died recently. Good thing they explained, or we and Jane wouldn't know what was going on, right?
- Jane knocks at the door of the house and asks to speak to the ladies, but Hannah is suspicious and doesn't want to let her talk to them, although she does offer her a piece of bread and a penny. She tells Jane to leave and bolts the door.
- Jane's too wet and hungry and exhausted to go anywhere, so she lets herself fall down on the doorstep and waits for God to decide what will happen to her.
- As Jane is lying on the doorstep, St. John arrives home and finds her there. Hannah still doesn't want to let Jane in, but St. John can tell that Jane isn't an ordinary beggar and invites her into the house.
- Diana and Mary are very sympathetic to Jane's plight; they offer her break and milk. Jane eats and drinks so fast that they have to take the food away so she doesn't make herself sick.
- Jane's too exhausted to tell her story, but she is quick-thinking enough to invent a pseudonym for herself – Jane Elliott.
- Even without knowing what's happened to Jane or why she's there, the three siblings agree to take care of her, and put her to bed in a spare room.

Volume III, Chapter Three

- For three days, Jane lies in the bed mostly unconscious while Diana, Mary, and Hannah take care of her. She does hear and understand some of the things that are said around her, and she hears the ladies discussing her and figuring out that she must be educated based on her accent, clothes, and facial features.
- St. John only comes into Jane's room once to look at her; he decides that she doesn't need a doctor, just rest, and analyzes her facial features a little more. (Once again, people are judging each other based on phrenology!)
- On the fourth day, Jane is able to sit up, talk, and even get dressed and go downstairs. She finds Hannah baking bread in the kitchen.
- Hannah is still suspicious of Jane and asks whether she's been a beggar before. Jane tells Hannah that, even though she doesn't have money or a home at the moment, she is educated and able to earn her keep, and plans to work again.

- Jane insists on helping Hannah with her work in the kitchen and asks Hannah questions about the family who has taken her in. She discovers that Diana, Mary, and St. John are siblings; their last name is Rivers; their mother has been dead for a long time; and their father died three weeks ago. Hannah has been the family's servant for thirty years and nursed all the children when they were young. Their house is called Moor House (or sometimes Marsh End).
- Once they're a little more comfortable with each other, Jane rebukes Hannah for thinking badly of her just because she's poor. She reminds Hannah that Christians don't consider poverty a crime, and they agree to be friends.
- Jane learns even more about the Rivers family from Hannah: they were once wealthy; Mrs. Rivers was highly educated and taught all her children to love learning; St. John is going to be a clergyman and his sisters are going to be governesses, because their father lost all his money.
- St. John, Diana, and Mary come home from their walk. The ladies insist that Jane come and sit with them in the parlor and have tea with them.
- While Diana and Mary get the tea, Jane is briefly left alone with St. John, who strikes her as an intense, harsh person.
- During tea, St. John cross-examines Jane about her background, even though his sisters object to his attitude. Jane tells him that she has no home, friends, or family, that she's never been married, and that she won't tell him where she last lived.
- St. John asks how he can help Jane if he doesn't know her story, and she tells him that all she really wants is work. He agrees to help her try to find a job.
- Jane decides to tell the Rivers siblings as much as possible about her life without giving away that she was at Thornfield or knew Mr. Rochester, so she tells them the short version of her autobiography. You know, school at Lowood as a pupil and a teacher, and then a position as a governess. She still won't tell them why she left her last job, although she says that she isn't at fault.
- Jane's almost home free when one of the sisters calls her "Miss Elliott," and her reaction proves that's not her real name. St. John notices, and Jane admits that it's a pseudonym.
- Diana and Mary are ready to pretty much adopt Jane into the family, but St. John is more interested in empowering her to earn her own living. For the moment, though, they agree that Jane can live with them.

Volume III, Chapter Four

- Jane continues to regain her strength living at Moor House. She's especially happy because, now that she's met Diana and Mary, she finally has some real friends of her own. The three women spend a lot of time together reading, talking, and walking on the moor. Diana starts teaching Jane German.
- Jane doesn't really develop a friendship with St. John. For one thing, he's not around a lot; he goes out visiting the sick and needy all the time, in all weathers. For another, he's a bit too reserved and cold to get friendly with her very fast.
- When Jane hears St. John preach, she's amazed at how powerful and intense he is, but also realizes that he's a really unhappy person.

- Diana and Mary prepare to move away and become governesses.
- Jane talks to St. John about the job he's promised to find for her. He says that he's been waiting until after his sisters leave to start their new jobs.
- St. John tells Jane about his family's poverty and warns her that he won't be able to get her a really great job, but he thinks she'll take what he found.
- St. John explains that he is the clergyman at the little town of Morton and that, when he came there two years ago, it didn't have a school. He established a boys' school and he's been meaning to establish a girls' school, too, funded by the rich factory owner in the town, Mr. Oliver. He asks Jane to run this school; she'll have a salary of thirty pounds a year (the same as at Thornfield!) and even a little house of her own beside the school.
- Jane accepts the post, which involves teaching village girls to read, write, do math, sew, and knit.
- Diana and Mary are very sad about having to leave; they might not see their brother again for a long time after they take up their new jobs.
- St. John gets a letter stating that the Rivers' Uncle John is dead. Jane watches as all the members of the Rivers family behave somewhat strangely about this – they're not exactly sad; she's not sure what they're feeling. St. John explains that their uncle had argued with their father long before, and that he had a fortune of twenty thousand pounds, but decided to leave all the money to another relative.

Volume III, Chapter Five

- Jane moves into her little cottage, which is simple but adequate.
- This was Jane's first day teaching at the new school; she had 20 students, only three of whom can read, so she's got her work cut out for her. She knows that she's doing really useful work, but she still feels like she's taken a step down on the social scale (which she has).
- Jane reminds herself that her current situation is better than being Rochester's mistress, but she doesn't seem to believe her own argument – she starts crying.
- St. John shows up, bringing Jane some drawing materials from his sisters. He asks how everything is going, and she says that it's wonderful, and she's grateful things are going so well for her when, a few days ago, she was homeless and friendless.
- St. John counsels Jane to keep trying to master her emotions and overcome her own desire to go back to whatever it is that she left. He tells her about his own experience denying himself – a year ago, he thought that he hated being a priest, but then he felt called by God to become a missionary. There's only one more desire he needs to overcome before he can go East, he says.
- A young woman comes up and wishes St. John good evening. St. John completely freaks out for a moment, but then calms himself down and turns to talk to her. Jane notices how beautiful the woman is.
- It turns out that this is Miss (Rosamond) Oliver, the daughter of the man who's paying Jane's salary. Miss Oliver says she'll come and help Jane out at the school sometimes.
- Miss Oliver tries to talk to St. John about normal things like a recent dance, but St. John is cold and disapproving.

- Miss Oliver gently teases St. John, saying that the dog, Carlo, would be more friendly to her. St. John blushes and his chest heaves, but he doesn't really respond.
- Miss Oliver invites St. John to come with her and see her father – she's on her way home – but St. John refuses. Miss Oliver thinks he's upset about his sisters leaving for their new jobs.

Volume III, Chapter Six

- Jane keeps teaching at the village school in Morton. At first it's really difficult work, but soon she starts making progress and feeling good about it. Everyone in the area seems to like her, which makes things even more pleasant.
- At night, however, Jane has weird dreams about Mr. Rochester.
- Rosamond Oliver goes to the school regularly, usually in the morning at the same time that St. John is there giving the girls a religious lesson. He blushes intensely and almost angrily when she comes in.
- Miss Oliver knows that St. John is in love with her – he doesn't hide it, but he refuses to act on his feelings. Rosamond pouts about this.
- Miss Oliver also visits Jane at her cottage. Jane decides that she is "coquettish, but not heartless; exacting, but not worthlessly selfish" (3.6.7) – which means that she's a little bit superficial and demanding, but not a bad person. Jane thinks she's a bit like Adèle (older, of course).
- Rosamond likes Jane and suspects that there's an exciting romantic story in her past. One evening, Rosamond goes through Jane's things and finds some French and German books and sketches.
- Rosamond asks Jane to do a portrait of her and Jane agrees.
- Jane gets to know Rosamond's father, Mr. Oliver, and the two of them comment on the fact that she seems smart enough to be a governess. Jane also learns that Mr. Oliver respects St. John and his family background, but thinks that St. John becoming a missionary is a waste.
- On a school holiday, Jane is sitting alone at home, finishing the picture of Rosamond Oliver, when St. John drops by to bring her a new book to read. When he sees the portrait, he becomes disturbed.
- Jane asks St. John about the portrait for a bit, and eventually he admits that he knows it's of Rosamond. She offers to make a copy for him – if he will admit that he wants one.
- St. John admits that he wants a copy of the picture, but says that it wouldn't be good for him to have it.
- Jane decides to play matchmaker. She knows Rosamond loves St. John, she knows St. John loves Rosamond, and she knows Rosamond's father would be OK with their marriage.
- St. John isn't angry – actually, he seems glad to be able to talk about it for once. He takes out his watch and puts it on the table, telling Jane that they can talk about Rosamond for fifteen minutes. He imagines what his life would be like if he decided to marry her and forget his plan of being a missionary.
- When the fifteen minutes are over, he stops thinking about this temptation. He tells Jane

that he knows Rosamond could never be a missionary's wife – she wouldn't like it, or be good at it. He knows that, on a practical level, he would regret marrying her.

- Jane reminds St. John how much he loves Rosamond – he blushes and shakes whenever she comes in the room. He tells her that's just a fleshly thing and that really he's a "cold, hard man."
- Jane doesn't believe him, and he tells her that, for example, he only takes an interest in her because she is hardworking and diligent – not because she suffered.
- St. John pulls a piece of scratch paper over the portrait so that he doesn't have to look at it anymore – and then he sees something on the scratch paper that really surprises him. Jane can't figure out what it is, but he tears off a piece and keeps it.

Volume III, Chapter Seven

- The next day, Jane sits in her cottage reading the book St. John brought her; it snowed all night and there are huge snowdrifts everywhere.
- St. John arrives, even though he had to struggle through the snow. He won't tell her why he's there, and he's behaving really strangely. She starts to worry that he might be a little bit insane.
- After a while, Jane goes back to reading, because St. John still won't tell her what's going on.
- Jane chats to St. John about various different things going on the village school, but he isn't really paying attention.
- Suddenly, St. John asks Jane to listen as he tells her a story that he's discovered:
- Twenty years before, a poor clergyman married a rich man's daughter and her family disowned her. Two years later they were both dead and left an orphan daughter.
- The orphan was adopted by Mrs. Reed of Gateshead and lived there for ten years.
- After ten years, the orphan went to Lowood Institute, and was a student and then a teacher there.
- After eight years at Lowood, the orphan became a governess for the ward of a man named Mr. Rochester.
- Rochester proposed to the girl, but at the altar it was revealed that his wife was alive and insane.
- The governess left in the middle of the night and nobody knows where she is, although they've been looking for her to tell her something important.
- Jane asks St. John how Mr. Rochester is, and he says he doesn't know – he just knows all the details that Mason's lawyer, Mr. Briggs, told him in a letter some time ago.
- St. John suggests that Mr. Rochester must have been "a bad man," but Jane denies this.
- St. John then shows Jane the thing he got so excited about the day before – her name, written on the piece of paper he tore off.
- Jane learns from St. John that Mr. Briggs is looking for her so that he can give her the fortune she inherited from her uncle, Mr. Eyre, who finally died out in Madeira. Jane can't quite wrap her head around all this. She finds out that she has inherited twenty thousand pounds.
- Before St. John leaves, Jane asks why Mr. Briggs wrote to him about her. He's reluctant

to tell her, but finally he admits that his name is St. John Eyre Rivers – his mother was the sister of Jane's father. Diana, Mary, and St. John are all Jane's cousins!

- Jane's much more excited about finding out that she has such great relatives than about the money. She realizes that she has the power to bring the Rivers family back together now that she has wealth – Diana and Mary won't have to be governesses anymore.
- St. John tries to talk Jane out of it, but she insists on splitting the twenty thousand pounds four ways so that she, St. John, Diana, and Mary each have five thousand.
- St. John also agrees to treat Jane as a sister, although he tells her that she doesn't have to feel like she's buying her family – she could keep the money. Jane still insists on splitting it.
- Jane agrees to stay at the village school until St. John finds a substitute, despite her newfound wealth.

Volume III, Chapter Eight

- At Christmastime, Jane closes up the school. St. John asks her if she feels good about the work she's been doing, and when she admits that she does he asks if she would devote her entire life to charitable works. She says that she couldn't do that; she wants to enjoy her own life, too.
- Jane begins preparing Moor House for Diana and Mary's return. St. John objects to her keeping her talents and abilities for her private domestic life and argues that she has larger duties in the world.
- Jane ignores St. John and spends a few days getting Moor House ready, cleaning and decorating.
- On the Thursday when Diana and Mary are supposed to arrive, Jane is waiting at the house for them. St. John arrives first; she shows him everything she's done in the house, but he doesn't care about any of it and starts reading a book.
- Jane realizes that St. John is right about his calling – he really doesn't care about leading a pleasant, comfortable life, only about huge, glorious projects and challenges and sacrifices.
- Diana and Mary arrive and are delighted with all Jane's work in the house.
- A poor boy comes and asks St. John to go and see his dying mother. St. John does and comes back tired but happier.
- Diana, Mary, and Jane spend Christmas week hanging out together and chatting; St. John gets away from them to do different clergyman-type duties as much as possible.
- Diana and Mary ask St. John about his plans; he has arranged to go to India next year, and he's heard that Rosamond Oliver is about to be married to someone else. Nobody really knows how to react to this, but St. John seems to be calm about it now.
- For a few weeks, things settle into a pattern; each of the women has something she's reading or studying, and Jane also makes weekly visits to the school. St. John is really excited about these weekly visits and encourages Jane to make them in all weathers.
- One day, St. John asks Jane to stop learning German and start learning Hindustani, because he needs a study-buddy and he thinks she would be better than either of his sisters. She agrees.

- Jane makes progress studying Hindustani, but somehow her teacher-student relationship with St. John makes her feel like she's very much under his control. She starts to be extremely obedient to him whenever he asks her to do anything.
- One evening, when St. John is kissing his sisters goodnight, Diana convinces him to kiss Jane, too, because she's sort of like a sister to them. He does, and the kiss is super-weird.
- More and more frequently, Jane wants to please St. John, but she feels like she has to suppress her real personality to do it.
- Jane writes to Mrs. Fairfax, but doesn't hear anything back from her.
- One day, St. John asks Jane to go for a walk with him. They go out onto the moor and sit beside some large rocks. St. John tells Jane about his plans to leave England for India in six weeks.
- St. John asks Jane to marry him and go with him to India; he says that God intended her to be a missionary's wife.
- Jane objects, saying that she doesn't have the right calling to be a missionary. St. John says that he's watched her for ten months (that's how long she's been in Morton), and he can tell she has all the right qualities.
- Jane asks for time to think, and they sit in silence. She realizes that she could do the work, but is worried that living in India would kill her. She also realizes that St. John might approve of her, but he'll never love her.
- Jane offers to go with St. John to India as his fellow-missionary, but refuses to marry him.
- St. John tries to persuade her that there's no way for her to go to India if she's not married to him; going alone together, both of them single, just wouldn't be right in his opinion.
- Jane sticks to her guns again. She'll go with him, but not as his wife. They can continue to be like brother and sister, since they are, after all, cousins, or even act just like co-workers.
- St. John refuses this arrangement again…they seem to be stuck in a loop here.
- St. John tells Jane that he's going to Cambridge for two weeks to say goodbye to various friends and that he wants her to think bout it while he's gone.
- That evening, they shake hands before going to bed; St. John is angry with her, although he thinks that he's forgiven her.

Volume III, Chapter Nine

- St. John stays at Moor House for another week. Jane feels tortured by his constant pressure, but the pressure just convinces her even more what a mistake it would be for her to actually marry him.
- The night before he leaves, Jane tries to get reconciled with him, but it just turns into the same argument: she refuses to marry him, and tells him that his weird behavior is killing her. He is incredibly angry.
- Jane offers again to go with St. John as his assistant, but not his wife. He insists that's absolutely impossible, but says that he'll arrange for her to go as the companion of some other missionary's wife. That way, he says, she won't be breaking her promise.
- Jane is outraged at the suggestion that she's made any formal agreement to go to India, especially with random strangers. She says that she won't leave England unless it's more

useful for her to leave than stay.

- St. John asks if Jane is going to see Rochester, and she admits it. They part.
- Jane goes back inside and sees Diana. Diana admits that she's been watching them from the window and asks what's been going on.
- Jane explains the situation to Diana: St. John doesn't love her, but has asked her to marry him and go with him to India. Diana is convinced that going to India would kill Jane because the climate is so harsh.
- Jane and Diana discuss St. John's offer of marriage. Diana agrees with Jane that she could never marry a man who just thought of her as "a useful tool," although she also defends her brother.
- Jane has to see St. John at dinner, and he behaves pretty normally. After dinner, during the family Bible reading, St. John chooses a freaky passage from the book of Revelations, and Jane realizes that he thinks she's damned.
- As St. John says good night to Jane, he tries again to convince her that marrying him and doing missionary work is God's will. Jane is awed by his manner and starts to relent – in fact, she's almost ready to agree to marry him!
- Suddenly, out of thin air, Jane hears Rochester's voice calling her name. She responds, but can't figure out where the voice is. Still, she breaks away from St. John and goes to her room to pray in her own way, eager to do something about what she's heard in the morning.

Volume III, Chapter Ten

- St. John slips a note under Jane's door in the morning; he can tell she was ready to sacrifice everything and become his wife and fellow missionary, and he'll ask her again when he comes back in two weeks.
- After St. John leaves, Jane thinks about the supernatural voice and wonders where it came from. She decides she must know what's going on with Rochester, wherever he is.
- Jane arranges a journey back to Thornfield; after 36 hours, she arrives at an inn called the Rochester Arms. She can't bring herself to ask anyone there about him, so she just starts walking to Thornfield.
- Jane comes up toward Thornfield walking along the wall of the orchard. She peeks out from around a corner of the wall – and sees a complete ruin. It's burned down, blackened and collapsed. She compares it to a man sneaking up to peek at the face of his sleeping beloved and finding her dead.
- Shocked, Jane goes back to the inn and asks the host what happened. From him she learns the whole story of what happened: Bertha burned down the house in the middle of the night by setting fire to what used to be Jane's own bed. Rochester saved the servants and then climbed up to a high wall where Bertha was standing to try and rescue her, but she jumped off and committed suicide. Rochester was blinded and lost a hand when the wall collapsed.
- Jane asks where Rochester is now, and the innkeeper tells her that he's at his other home, Ferndean. Jane arranges to go there in a chaise right away.

Volume III, Chapter Eleven

- Jane goes to Ferndean to find Rochester. When she comes up to the house, she sees him coming out, and watches him for a long time without letting him know she's there. He looks like "some wronged and fettered wild beast or bird, dangerous to approach in his sullen woe" – in other words, he's really let himself go.
- Jane goes into the house and talks to the servants, John and Mary. She arranges to bring a tray in to Rochester in Mary's place.
- When Jane enters the parlor, the dog, Pilot recognizes her. Rochester realizes something is up and demands to know what's going on, but he doesn't know it's Jane yet.
- Rochester reaches out, trying to touch her, and she takes his hand in hers. When he feels her fingers, he clasps her to him and figures out who she is based on her shape. Sexy, eh?
- Rochester can hardly believe that it's really Jane, but when she tells him about her inheritance he decides this is reality – he would never imagine something boring about wills and money.
- Jane offers to be Rochester's nurse or housekeeper, convinced that he will immediately ask her to marry him again, but he doesn't.
- Jane insists that Rochester eat supper, which he usually doesn't. They eat and talk together, but Jane won't tell him yet where she was or what she was doing. Rochester's still worried that she's a spirit or ghost or hallucination. Jane combs his hair, which he's allowed to get a bit wild.
- Jane heads to bed without answering any of Rochester's questions. She decides to tease him for a while and let him think she fell in love with someone else in order to distract him from his depression.
- In the morning, Jane comes down to breakfast, and then takes Rochester outside so they can stroll in the wood and meadows.
- They sit down in a dry place and Rochester asks Jane to tell him where she's been and what's happened to her. She tells the story, but doesn't emphasize how hungry she got during the first three days.
- When Jane tells Rochester about Moor House, he cross-examines her about St. John Rivers. Jane answers with the truth, but very sparingly, and he becomes convinced that she's in love with St. John.
- When Jane finally reveals that she has no feelings for St. John – and that St. John was only interested in her because she'd be a good missionary's wife – Rochester is ecstatic. He laments his blindness and lost hand, but asks Jane to marry him anyway. She accepts gladly.
- Rochester is worried that Jane will find it unpleasant to wait on him and deal with his blindness, but she says she's even more happy to be his wife now, when she can be really useful to him.
- As they walk back to the house for dinner, Rochester tells Jane that he understands why she had to leave him, and that he feels remorse and repentance for his behavior in the past.
- Rochester also tells Jane that, four days before, between eleven and twelve at night, he called her name three times frantically – *and he heard her respond*. He thinks that perhaps

they met in spirit.
- Jane doesn't tell Rochester that she heard him call her name and responded to him while she was sitting, miles away, with St. John. She doesn't want him to get obsessed with the supernatural.

Volume III, Chapter Twelve

- Jane and Rochester have a quiet wedding; the servants are surprised, but they approve.
- Jane tells the Rivers siblings about her wedding; St. John doesn't write to her for six months.
- Adèle goes to one boarding school and then another because Jane doesn't have time to teach her; the English schools seem to take the French-ness out of her and she becomes less frivolous.
- Jane and Rochester live happily ever after; the Jane telling the story has been married to Mr. Rochester for ten years.
- Rochester gets his sight back after two years of marriage.
- Jane and Rochester have a son.
- Diana and Mary Rivers each get married.
- St. John Rivers goes to India alone and works himself to death there. The novel ends with a quotation from one of his letters in which he anticipates his own death.

Themes

Theme of Marriage

In *Jane Eyre*, marriage is about a combination of three things: compatibility, passion, and ethics. A marriage only works between like-minded individuals with similar attitudes and outlooks on life. Inequalities of class background or financial situation are surmountable, but characters who marry for wealth or status are doomed. But a marriage has to have more than common ground – it has to have passion. Characters who try to match themselves up based on rational criteria, the ones who are doing nineteenth-century-style online dating, sin against their own natures, as do characters who try to claim that marriage and love are the same thing.

Questions About Marriage

1. What are the different marriages that *Jane Eyre,* as a novel, explores as possibilities? What makes each of these pairings likely or unlikely?
2. Are any of Rochester's arguments that his relationship with Bertha isn't really a "marriage" persuasive? Why or why not?
3. At what point in the novel does it become clear that a marriage between Jane and Rochester is possible? Why? At what point in the novel does their marriage become

desirable? Why? What's the difference?
4. Why does Jane refuse to marry St. John Rivers?
5. How would Jane, as a character, be different if she did marry St. John and go with him to India?

Chew on Marriage

Rochester's relationship with Bertha Mason is no longer really a marriage, and he should not be considered ethically bound to her as a husband.

Rochester's attempt to convince Jane to elope with him while Bertha is still living results from his redefinition of marriage in terms of interpersonal sympathy rather than a social contract.

Theme of Education

In *Jane Eyre*, education provides the only route for someone who isn't independently wealthy to improve their character and prospects – it allows social mobility. The "education" we're talking about in this novel, however, is mostly aesthetic; characters learn basic music performance, basic artistic skills, and a little bit of foreign language. It's enough to make them seem cultured, but not to make them actually useful for anything except teaching music, art, and foreign language. Education is also a safe haven, something that provides emotional satisfaction in a protected space separate from the hardships of the world.

Questions About Education

1. Why does Jane want to go to school or learn anything in the first place? Why does education become such an important issue for her as a child?
2. What does Jane's formal education at Lowood prepare her to do?
3. What does Jane's *informal* education at Lowood consist of, and what does it prepare her for?
4. At what points in the novel does Jane value learning for its own sake, and why? At what points does she value learning for other reasons – and what are they?
5. Does education replace something else in Jane's life? If so, what?
6. Jane makes her living as an educator – a teacher or a governess. Is there a sense in which Jane's most important relationships – with Rochester, St. John, Mrs. Reed, and others – are all related to her profession somehow?

Chew on Education

In Jane's childhood, education takes the place of every single one of her emotional and physical needs – food, shelter, family, and friendship.

Because Jane initially learns to understand the world in terms of a teacher-student relationship, all her friendships have some master-pupil tinge to them.

Theme of Appearances

Appearances are almost always inversely related to the actual nature of the characters in *Jane Eyre*. Beautiful women turn out to be scheming harpies or selfish idiots; plain women turn out to have hidden depths of passion; ugly men aren't actually ugly, but excitingly masculine in a harsh, craggy way. Virtuous characters resist having their appearances radically changed or improved because doing so seems like pretending to be something they aren't. In contrast, characters who let themselves get obsessed with keeping external appearances plain and modest are distracted from deeper spiritual truths and often turn out to be hypocritical anyway.

Questions About Appearances

1. Is Jane actually plain-looking? Think about this for a moment. Which characters claim that Jane is plain or ugly? Which characters describe her as beautiful, and when? (Think especially about Jane's time at Moor House in Book III.)
2. Why does the novel need to show us the plainly-dressed girls at Lowood and the dolled-up Brocklehurst women in Book I? What is the reader being prepared to understand later on?
3. What does Bertha Mason actually look like? Who does she look like – to which other character does Rochester compare her?
4. Are appearances deceptive in *Jane Eyre*?
5. Are there clear correspondences between moral nature and appearance in this novel or not?

Chew on Appearances

Jane's claim that she is a "plain, Quakerish governess" is actually somewhat misleading; her attempt to hide her beauty from the reader demonstrates her belief that beauty and morality are mutually exclusive.

Although other characters occasionally claim that Jane is beautiful, her beauty is always related to her mood or her character; it's an "inner beauty" that the reader can only understand because Jane is a "plain, Quakerish governess" on the outside.

Theme of Society and Class

Jane Eyre (the novel, not the character) looks down its nose in disgust at the existing Victorian class hierarchy. The characters who are most interested in the trappings of wealth and status are hypocritical or morally misguided, but characters who take poverty on themselves to demonstrate their great moral nature are also mocked. Instead of the normal class structures, *Jane Eyre* implies that poverty can be thoroughly respectable, as long as it's accompanied by an earnest desire to better oneself – or at least earn one's keep. Of course, it's easy to value poverty and hard work when, in the end, all the right people get the money.

Questions About Society and Class

1. Where does Jane seem to stand in the social hierarchy? Does she have social mobility, or

does her class status remain relatively constant?

2. As a novel, how does *Jane Eyre* depict high society and wealthy aristocrats? What are their virtues? What are their flaws?
3. How do Jane's attitudes toward poverty and the poor change over the course of the novel? How does religion factor into this attitude change?
4. Why does Jane have to become destitute before she can become wealthy?
5. Why is it important for Jane to inherit wealth of her own before she marries Rochester?

Chew on Society and Class

In *Jane Eyre*, it is easier for characters to be morally pure if they are poor or if they refuse or renounce possible wealth.

Jane's inheritance brings with it financial freedom and personal independence; without these, she would not be able to bring herself to marry Rochester, because in doing so she would become his dependent.

Theme of The Supernatural

There are very few things in *Jane Eyre* that are actually supernatural, but the supernatural is still a major theme in this novel. How can that be? Over and over, events that seem eerie, uncanny, Gothic, or supernatural will be explained away by rational circumstances. But here's the kicker: those rational explanations will turn out to be far more sinister than anything otherworldly. We'd tell you more, but we don't want to spoil it. Oh, and those few things that *are* actually supernatural? Well, they add an interesting layer of ambiguity to the novel at the very beginning and the very end.

Questions About The Supernatural

1. Are there any supernatural elements in *Jane Eyre* that don't get explained away with rational facts? This is a source of some debate among critics, but we'll give you a hint: there are two things, one toward the beginning of the novel and one toward the end, that could be genuinely supernatural. What are they and why are they important?
2. Why does the novel explain away most of its seemingly supernatural elements? To think of it another way, why couldn't *Jane Eyre* actually have the ghost of Mr. Reed appear and speak to Jane, or Bertha Mason really be Dracula's cousin one bite removed?
3. If *Jane Eyre* explains away almost all of the things that seem supernatural in the novel, then why are there supernatural things in it at all? Why does the novel tease us by making us think there might be ghosts or vampires or haunted houses when it turns out they aren't there?
4. Why is Rochester always calling Jane a fairy or an elf or a sprite? Is there anything about her that actually seems uncanny or otherworldly? Is he just being ironic because she's so plain and down to earth?

Chew on The Supernatural

Jane Eyre uses supernatural imagery, but not actual supernatural elements, in order to create a mood and tone of Gothic horror in the context of social realism.

Jane's characterization in terms of elfin or fairy-like qualities creates a dark, eerie undertone to her usually staid and proper exterior.

Theme of Morality and Ethics

In the strictest sense, *Jane Eyre* is all about morality – in fact, it's close to being didactic (it's as if Brontë was trying to teach her readers about ethics). Characters seem to have an innate sense of right and wrong, and it isn't difficult to tell what decision to make in an ethical crisis. It is, however, extremely difficult for these characters to make ethical choices in a world where morality and passion seem to be mutually exclusive. Characters must choose between being right and being happy. Luckily, in the end, circumstances will conspire to get all the ethical obstacles out of the way so that we can have the happy ending we've been craving.

Questions About Morality and Ethics

1. Does Jane learn her morality from Helen Burns at Lowood, or does she have an innate moral sense of her own that exists before she meets Helen?
2. Does Helen change Jane's mind about what ethical behavior really is, or do Helen and Jane disagree about ethics?
3. Is Rochester an immoral person or was he just completely screwed by his circumstances?
4. What is the reader's relationship to the central moral issue of *Jane Eyre*, Rochester's attempt to marry Jane while he already was married to Bertha? Where and with whom do our sympathies lie?
5. Is *Jane Eyre* a preachy moral tale that teaches us to respect the rules, or does it make us feel uncomfortable with the rules and think that moral principles could vary, relative to different situations?
6. When Jane returns to Rochester at the end of the novel, is her decision a moral one, or is it an emotional one? If it is a moral decision (and it might not be!), then is the moral issue her relationship with Mr. Rochester, or her relationship with St. John Rivers?

Chew on Morality and Ethics

Jane's decision to abandon Rochester when she discovers that Bertha is living creates a separation between her and the reader; while Jane chooses ethics over passion, the reader is caught up in the romantic plot, rooting for love to triumph over everything, even morality.

The true "moral lesson" for Jane is not that it would be unethical for her to be Rochester's mistress, but that it would be unethical for her to be St. John Rivers' wife.

Theme of Foreignness and 'The Other'

Foreignness and 'The Other' are complex themes in *Jane Eyre*. The novel depends heavily on the relationship between England, at the center, and a variety of other places and groups: colonial holdings, continental nations, missionary outposts, and even oriental stereotypes. England and Englishness are both strengthened and threatened by each of these factors, and the ability to move between the foreign and the domestic is an opportunity for financial and personal gain – but also a chance for contamination, threats, fear, or prejudice. Even characters who seem to be at the very center of England and the very center of the novel can easily be made to seem foreign and out of place.

Questions About Foreignness and 'The Other'

1. There are a lot of different countries outside England that play important roles in *Jane Eyre* , especially France, India, and Jamaica. What is the novel's tone or attitude toward each of these places? What do they represent or get stereotyped as representing?
2. How can we, as twenty-first-century readers, think critically and productively about the racism and prejudice that are obvious in a nineteenth-century novel like *Jane Eyre*? Is it enough to say that historical context explains these attitudes, or do we need to delve deeper into them to understand how they work?
3. How does Bertha's Creole heritage relate to other aspects of her characterization?
4. How would the novel be different if Bertha was a white Englishwoman or if Jane was Creole?
5. Does Jane herself get "othered" in the context of *Jane Eyre*? In what settings does she seem like an outsider or a foreigner?

Chew on Foreignness and 'The Other'

Bertha Mason embodies all the things that threaten the landed Victorian gentry: feminine sexuality, racial otherness, irrational behavior, and overseas wealth.

Jane's outsider status at Gateshead is similar to Bertha's outsider status at Thornfield.

Theme of The Home

In one sense, *Jane Eyre* is about the quest of an orphan girl for a home. In this novel, home isn't just where you hang your hat – it has to be somewhere that you not only feel comfortable and safe, but also have loving relationships with other people. It's even possible for characters to be metaphorically homeless here even though they've lived in the same place their whole lives. It's also possible for characters to have more than one home because they have different family and romantic relationships that create several comfortable refuges for them.

Questions About The Home

1. What is a "home" in this novel?
2. When and where does Jane feel "at home," and why? (Hint: there's more than one place

that Jane calls home in the course of the novel.)
3. What does Jane mean when she says to Rochester that he is her home? What about Rochester makes her feel this way? (Hint: think about where Jane and Rochester are in the scene where she makes this comment.)
4. Why might it be important for Jane to have a time, however brief, when she lives alone in a house of her own?
5. Why is it important for Jane to have a period of literal homelessness?
6. Why does Jane tend to seek refuge outside – either in the garden, in the woods, or on the moor – rather than inside? (Hint: this is relevant to all of the places she lives.)

Chew on The Home

Jane conceives of "home" as an emotional place created by interpersonal relationships, not as a physical shelter.

Jane tends to feel more at home outside than inside because the natural world has provided her with more of a refuge than any human habitation.

Quotes

Marriage Quotes

"He is not to them what he is to me," I thought: "he is not of their kind. I believe he is of mine; – I am sure he is, – I feel akin to him, – I understand the language of his countenance and movements: though rank and wealth sever us widely, I have something in my brain and heart, in my blood and nerves, that assimilates me mentally to him. [...] I must, then, repeat continually that we are for ever sundered: – and yet, while I breathe and think I must love him." (2.2.85)

Thought: Seeing Rochester among his high-class houseguests, Jane realizes that he has more in common with her than he does with them. Despite Jane's and Rochester's different class backgrounds, their master-servant relationship, and the strict gender roles of Victorian society, Jane can tell that they share something intangible – but she doubts that they can overcome all the social obstacles keeping them apart. This isn't the first time Jane has felt affection for someone – but it may be the first time she's felt *like* somebody else.

"Whenever I marry," she continued, after a pause which none interrupted, "I am resolved my husband shall not be a rival, but a foil to me. I will suffer no competitor near the throne; I shall exact an undivided homage: his devotions shall not be shared between me and the shape he sees in his mirror." (2.2.128)

Thought: Blanche Ingram's idea of a good marriage is one in which the partners are distinctly different and one partner is far superior to the other. As a stunning beauty, she doesn't want a handsome husband, but a hideous one – that way she'll always get all the attention. Notice how different this is from Jane's (and Rochester's) ideas about love and marriage--they're drawn together because they are alike. Blanche thinks that opposites attract, but Jane knows that kindred spirits attract more strongly.

Ere long, a bell tinkled, and the curtain drew up. Within the arch, the bulky figure of Sir George Lynn, whom Mr. Rochester had likewise chosen, was seen enveloped in a white sheet: before him, on a table, lay open a large book; and at his side stood Amy Eshton, draped in Mr. Rochester's cloak, and holding a book in her hand. Somebody, unseen, rang the bell merrily; then Adèle (who had insisted on being one of her guardian's party) bounded forward, scattering round her the contents of a basket of flowers she carried on her arm. Then appeared the magnificent figure of Miss Ingram, clad in white, a long veil on her head, and a wreath of roses round her brow: by her side walked Mr. Rochester, and together they drew near the table. They knelt; while Mrs. Dent and Louisa Eshton, dressed also in white, took up their stations behind them. A ceremony followed, in dumb show, in which it was easy to recognize the pantomime of a marriage. (2.3.8)

Thought Blanche Ingram and Mr. Rochester pair up for an elaborate game of charades, and the first thing they do is play-act their own wedding, silently, in front of the other houseguests and Jane. This is the first of several not-quite-real weddings we'll see in *Jane Eyre*, each of which suggests something about the actual marriages and pairings in the novel. In this particular case, the pretend wedding is meant to be a charade for the word "bride" – but that's only the first half of the word being acted out in the game, which is "Bridewell," a famous prison. Hmm, something that begins with a marriage ends with being in prison. Do you think that's supposed to be some kind of OMEN or something?

I saw he was going to marry her, for family, perhaps political reasons; because her rank and connexions suited him; I felt he had not given her his love, and that her qualifications were ill adapted to win from him that treasure. This was the point – this was where the nerve was touched and teazed – this was where the fever was sustained and fed: she could not charm him . (2.3.27, italics original)

Thought: Jane is really hot and bothered by the idea that Rochester is going to marry Blanche, not just because she's jealous, but also because she can tell that they are so unsuited and that Rochester himself knows exactly how flawed and unpleasant Blanche is. Jane herself knows exactly how to "charm" Rochester, how to argue with him and keep him amused and even how make him love her. Basically, the way Jane feels here is the way we feel when we see someone doing something badly that we know how to do well. She wants to take Rochester away and show Blanche how this relationship should be done – but she can't. She has to watch and suffer in silence, as usual.

I have not yet said anything condemnatory of Mr. Rochester's project of marrying for interest and connexions. [...] All their class held these principles: I supposed, then, they had reasons for holding them such as I could not fathom. It seemed to me that, were I a gentleman like him, I would take to my bosom only such a wife as I could love; but the very obviousness of the advantages to the husband's own happiness, offered by this plan, convinced me that there must be arguments against its general adoption of which I was quite ignorant: otherwise I felt sure all the world would act as I wished to act. (2.3.31)

Thought: Jane doesn't get why anyone would *not* marry for love, especially if they're rich enough to do pretty much whatever they want, but she figures there must be some reason that so many people who are already wealthy and important insist on marrying to get more money and status instead of to make themselves happy. Notice that Jane doesn't talk about her own ideas about marriage – only the ideas that she would have if she were in Rochester's place. Somehow Jane can't conceive of *herself* needing to make a choice about marrying for love or status – only of a man like Rochester doing so.

"What tale do you like best to hear?"

"Oh, I have not much choice! They generally run on the same theme – courtship; and promise to end in the same catastrophe – marriage."

"And do you like that monotonous theme?"

"Positively, I don't care about it: it is nothing to me." (2.4.49-52)

Thought: You remember what's going on here, right? Rochester, disguised as the old gypsy woman, is trying to get Jane to admit that she's in love with him. (Go back and read the summary of Book II, Chapter Four if you have no idea what we're talking about.) The real question here is, do we believe Jane's claim that marriage is "nothing" to her and that she doesn't care about it? We already know that she's in love with Rochester, but we also know that she thinks that relationship isn't going anywhere.

"Come to my side, Jane, and let us explain and understand one another."

"I will never again come to your side: I am torn away now, and cannot return."

"But, Jane, I summon you as my wife: it is you only I intend to marry."

I was silent: I thought he mocked me.

"Come, Jane – come hither."

"Your bride stands between us."

He rose, and with a stride reached me.

"My bride is here," he said, again drawing me to him, "because my equal is here, and my likeness. Jane, will you marry me?" (2.8.80-87)

Thought: Fair warning: we could have picked almost any quote from Book II, Chapter 8, because it's pretty much all like this. The irony is thick on the ground here – as Jane will learn at the end of Book II, Rochester's bride does indeed stand between them, but it's not Blanche Ingram! Notice that Rochester claims a woman could only qualify as his "bride" if she is also his "equal" and "likeness." He's laying the groundwork for twisting this argument around later in the novel and claiming that a woman who isn't his "likeness" can't be his wife no matter what anyone (even the law) says.

"That is my wife," said he. "Such is the sole conjugal embrace I am ever to know – such are the endearments which are to solace my leisure hours! And this is what I wished to have" (laying his hand on my shoulder): "this young girl, who stands so grave and quiet at the mouth of hell, looking collectedly at the gambols of a demon. I wanted her just as a change after that fierce ragout. Wood and Briggs, look at the difference! Compare these clear eyes with the red balls yonder – this face with that mask – this form with that bulk; then judge me, priest of the Gospel and man of the law, and remember, with what judgement ye judge ye shall be judged!" (2.11.80)

Thought: Rochester has admitted that he was trying to commit bigamy, but the weird part is that we kind of sympathize with him. The contrast between Bertha, the wild and crazy vampire-ish woman, and plain little Jane the "Quakerish governess" really makes us understand what Rochester is saying: Bertha's really not playing the role of a wife in his life, so why shouldn't he be allowed to marry Jane, especially because she's so awesome? Then we stop for a minute and think, whoa, we're not exactly on board with this, because it's not really fair to Jane. But we do feel bad for the guy.

"It is strange," pursued he, "that while I love Rosamond Oliver so wildly – with all the intensity, indeed, of a first passion, the object of which is exquisitely beautiful, graceful, fascinating – I experience at the same time a calm, unwarped consciousness that she would not make me a good wife; that she is not the partner suited to me; that I should discover this within a year after marriage; and that to twelve months' rapture would succeed a lifetime of regret. This I know." (3.6.45)

Thought: St. John's radical separation of his emotional attachment to Rosamond from his calm, collected assessment of what a good wife is sounds pretty good at first – and really similar, in some ways, to Jane's rejection of Rochester. But something's bothering us about it. Oh, right, it's the implication that he's (someday) going to marry a woman he doesn't love. On purpose. Now that's masochistic.

"Consent, then, to his demand is possible: but for one item – one dreadful item. It is – that he asks me to be his wife, and has no more of a husband's heart for me than that frowning giant of a rock, down which the stream is foaming in yonder gorge. He prizes me as a soldier would a good weapon; and that is all. Unmarried to him, this would never grieve me; but can I let him complete his calculations – coolly put into practice his plans – go through the wedding ceremony? Can I receive from him the bridal ring, endure all the forms of love (which I doubt not he would scrupulously observe) and know that the spirit was quite absent? Can I bear the

consciousness that every endearment he bestows is a sacrifice made on principle? No: such a martyrdom would be monstrous. I will never undergo it. As his sister, I might accompany him – not as his wife: I will tell him so." (3.8.116)

Thought: The (imaginary, thank goodness) spectacle of St. John forcing himself to have sex with Jane even though he doesn't love her and she doesn't love him is nauseating. Clearly, a marriage can't be conducted simply based on a rational analysis of which people are compatible as "help-meets." St. John's legalistic ideas about marriage make Rochester's fast-and-loose proposals look positively squeaky-clean by comparison.

Education Quotes

Each picture told a story; mysterious often to my undeveloped understanding and imperfect feelings, yet ever profoundly interesting: as interesting as the tales Bessie sometimes narrated on winter evenings, when she chanced to be in good humour; and when, having brought her ironing-table to the nursery-hearth, she allowed us to sit about it, and while she got up Mrs. Reed's lace frills, and crimped her night-cap borders, fed our eager attention with passages of love and adventure taken from the old fairy tales and older ballads; or (as at a later period I discovered) from the pages of Pamela, and Henry, Earl of Moreland. (1.1.13)

Thought: Very early in her life, stories, tales, and narratives are some of the most positive things that Jane experiences. It's unsurprising that she becomes a teacher and governess, given that hearing tales from her nursemaid was a special treat, and that these tales naturally segue into hearing parts of, and then reading, novels. (By the way, we definitely recommend *Pamela*.) Even at the very beginning of the novel, Jane is learning to be an astute "reader" of the pictures in *Bewick's British Birds* , and to connect the text with the pictures to understand what's going on.

I scarcely knew what school was; Bessie sometimes spoke of it as a place where young ladies sat in the stocks, wore backboards, and were expected to be exceedingly genteel and precise; John Reed hated his school, and abused his master: but John Reed's tastes were no rule for mine, and if Bessie's accounts of school-discipline (gathered from the young ladies of a family where she had lived before coming to Gateshead) were somewhat appalling, her details of certain accomplishments attained by these same ladies were, I thought, equally attractive. She boasted of beautiful paintings of landscapes and flowers by them executed; of songs they could sing and pieces they could play, of purses they could net, of French books they could translate; till my spirit was moved to emulation as I listened. Besides, school would be a complete change: it implied a long journey, an entire separation from Gateshead, an entrance into a new life. (1.3.70)

Thought: Jane instinctively embraces the opportunity to go to school – it's a way to get away from Gateshead, and the fact that people she hates dislike school probably means that she'll enjoy it. It's sort of an "enemy of my enemy is my friend" thing. She's also really interested in being "accomplished," in learning, and in being a talented, cultured person, which is more than we can say for any of the Reeds. From the beginning, then, Jane's motives for getting an education are complex: she loves learning for its own sake, but it's also a way out of a bad living situation, and a way to distinguish herself from louts like John.

I had meant to be so good, and to do so much at Lowood; to make so many friends, to earn respect, and win affection. Already I had made visible progress: that very morning I had reached the head of my class; Miss Miller had praised me warmly; Miss Temple had smiled approbation; she had promised to teach me drawing, and to let me learn French, if I continued to make similar improvement two months longer: and then I was well-received by my fellow-pupils; treated as an equal by those of my own age, and not molested by any: now, here I lay again crushed and trodden on; and could I ever rise more? (1.8.1)

Thought: From her first days at Lowood, Jane sees learning not only as something enjoyable (she thinks learning French is a special treat!) but as her way of rising in the world and earning friends and approval. Still, learning doesn't make up for ethics, and Jane is very defensive about being slandered.

They conversed of things I had never heard of; of nations and times past; of countries far away: of secrets of nature discovered or guessed at: they spoke of books: how many they had read! What stores of knowledge they possessed! Then they seemed so familiar with French names and French authors: but my amazement reached its climax when Miss Temple asked Helen if she sometimes snatched a moment to recall the Latin her father had taught her, and taking a book from a shelf, bade her read and construe a page of Virgil; and Helen obeyed, my organ of Veneration expanding at every sounding line. (1.8.52)

Thought: At this moment, Jane develops a love of knowledge and learning that has something to do with the sparkling conversation going on between Miss Temple and Helen Burns, but a lot more to do with the way that she idolizes the two of them. Just like a girl watching her idols today, Jane wants to be what they are – but instead of having fashion mavens like Tyra Banks for idols, she has a schoolteacher and a pious little girl. But the main impulse is the same – Jane basically hero-worships both of them and everything they do.

Thus relieved of a grievous load, I from that hour set to work afresh, resolved to pioneer my way through every difficulty: I toiled hard, and my success was proportionate to my efforts; my memory, not naturally tenacious, improved with practice; exercise sharpened my wits; in a few weeks I was promoted to a higher class; in less than two months I was allowed to commence French and drawing. I learned the first two tenses of the verb Être, and sketched my first cottage…on the same day. That night, on going to bed, I forgot to prepare in imagination the Barmecide supper of hot roast potatoes, or white break and new milk, with which I was wont to amuse my inward cravings: I feasted instead on the spectacle of ideal drawings, which I saw in the dark; all the work of my own hands… (1.8.59)

Thought: When Jane starts fantasizing about homework instead of food, we get a tiny bit nervous about her. Still, we're glad that she's found something to sustain her through the long, cold, hungry nights at Lowood.

I had had no communication by letter or message with the outer world: school-rules, school-duties, school-habits and notions, and voices, and faces, and phrases, and costumes, and preferences, and antipathies: such was what I knew of existence. And now I felt that it was not enough: I tired of the routine of eight years in one afternoon. I desired liberty... (1.10.9)

Thought: Some people get sick of things slowly and stuff builds up forever; other people wake up one day and need to change their whole lives. Obviously, Jane is the second type of person. It's pretty amazing, though, that she realizes there's more to life than studying – after all, education was her ticket out of Gateshead and her way of earning approval from her closest friends and teachers. Where do you think Jane got the idea that education is only a part of her life, and not the whole of it? Why does she get sick of Lowood and long to get out in the world, besides simple wanderlust?

"I dare say you are clever, though," continued Bessie, by way of solace. "What can you do? Can you play on the piano?"

"A little."

There was one in the room; Bessie went and opened it, and then asked me to sit down and give her a tune: I played a waltz or two and she was charmed.

"The Miss Reeds could not play as well!" she said exultingly. "I always said you would surpass them in learning." (1.10.66-69)

Thought: Bessie has always thought of Jane's intellectual abilities as making up for, or even replacing, her (lack of) good looks. If Bessie were a high school teacher, she'd be the kind who totally believed that there are only two kinds of girls: popular pretty ones, and dorky bookish ones, and never the twain shall meet. We know that's a pretty silly way to see the world – haven't we learned from reality TV that anyone can be gorgeous with the right expensive makeover? And haven't you learned from Shmoop that anyone can get smarter with the right tutor? It's nice that Bessie's so excited for Jane's accomplishments, but the way she sees the world – pretty and smart are opposites – is going to make a lot of trouble for Jane down the line, when she has to keep herself dowdy in order to feel savvy.

"Oh, don't fall back on over-modesty! I have examined Adèle, and find you have taken great pains with her: she is not bright, she has no talents; yet in a short time she has made much improvement."

"Sir, you have given me my 'cadeau'; I am obliged to you: it is the meed teachers most covet; praise of their pupils' progress." (1.13.30-31)

Thought: This little moment where Rochester tells Jane she's a good teacher is important, because Jane never tells us so herself. It's one of the things she forgets to mention, or maybe leaves out – her modesty is getting in the way of telling her own story. It won't be the last time that Jane can't be trusted to depict herself accurately.

I could talk a while when the evening commenced: but the first gush of vivacity and fluency gone, I was fain to sit on a stool at Diana's feet, to rest my head on her knee, and listen alternately to her and Mary; while they sounded thoroughly the topic on which I had but touched. Diana offered to teach me German. I liked to learn of her: I saw the part of instructress pleased and suited her; that of scholar pleased and suited me no less. (3.4.4)

Thought: In her refuge at Moor House, Jane reverts to her Lowood days; Diana is a lot like Miss Temple and Helen Burns combined, a kind and intelligent teacher who also has strong religious beliefs. During this difficult moment, Jane becomes a student – and a child – all over again in order to recuperate after her traumatic experience with Rochester.

This morning, the village school opened. I had twenty scholars. But three of the number can read: none write or cipher. Several knit, and a few sew a little. They speak with the broadest accent of the district. At present, they and I have a difficulty in understanding each other's language. Some of them are unmannered, rough, intractable, as well as ignorant; but others are docile, have a wish to learn, and evince a disposition that pleases me. I must not forget that these coarsely-clad little peasants are of flesh and blood as good as the scions of gentlest genealogy; and that the germs of native excellence, refinement, intelligence, kind feeling, are as likely to exist in their hearts as in those of the best-born. My duty will be to develop these germs: surely I shall find some happiness in discharging that office. (3.5.2)

Thought: Basically, this is the part where the new college grad with a degree in education (Jane) has turned down a gig at a high-class private school (tutoring Adèle) in order to do Teach for America (the village school). It's her community service time, something way more difficult and way more low-to-the-ground than she was trained for, but she can feel good about it.

Appearances Quotes

Bessie, when she heard this narrative, sighed and said, "Poor Miss Jane is to be pitied, too, Abbot."

"Yes," responded Abbot, "if she were a nice, pretty child, one might compassionate her forlornness; but one really cannot care for such a little toad as that."

"Not a great deal, to be sure," agreed Bessie: "at any rate a beauty like Miss Georgiana would be more moving in the same condition."

"Yes, I doat on Miss Georgiana!" cried the fervent Abbot. "Little darling! – with her long curls and her blue eyes, and such a sweet colour as she has; just as if she were painted!" (1.3.77-80)

Thought: Jane Eyre is famous for being a plain-looking girl rather than a beauty, and here we see the unfortunate and unfair consequences of her plainness: the servants find it difficult to sympathize with her just because she's not cute and sweet and blue-eyed and curly-haired. Compassion and affection are easier for people like Bessie and Abbot to give to pretty girls. Yeah, they're not shallow or anything.

"Miss Temple, Miss Temple, what – what is that girl with curled hair? Red hair, ma'am, curled – curled all over?" And extending his cane he pointed to the awful object, his hand shaking as he did so.

"It is Julia Severn," replied Miss Temple, very quietly.

"Julia Severn, ma'am! And why has she, or any other, curled hair? Why, in defiance of every precept and principle of this house, does she conform to the world so openly – here in an evangelical, charitable establishment – as to wear her hair one mass of curls?"

"Julia's hair curls naturally," returned Miss Temple, still more quietly.

"Naturally! Yes, but we are not to conform to nature: I wish these girls to be the children of Grace: and why that abundance? I have again and again intimated that I desire the hair to be arranged closely, modestly, plainly. Miss Temple, that girl's hair must be cut off entirely […]." (1.7.23-27)

Thought: Poor Julia Severn. Here we see Mr. Brocklehurst at his most unreasonable. Later, he'll claim that the girls at Lowood Institution shouldn't curl or braid their hair because that's wasting time on worldly vanities. OK, that's a little extreme, but we understand the logic: just take what you're given and don't worry about your appearance. But here he implies that, if Julia can't find a way to straighten her hair and make it less good-looking, then he'll give her one serious buzz cut. So he's contradicting himself: if curls are bad because they're an unnatural kind of ornament, then Julia's, which are natural, should be OK. But here he freaks out and claims that "we are not to conform to nature" and that the girls should live under Grace (that's the grace of God, if you're following) instead. But didn't God give Julia her curly hair? Why does Mr. Brocklehurst try to say that nature and Grace are different, then? That's right, he's an idiot.

"I have a Master to serve whose kingdom is not of this world: my mission is to mortify in these girls the lusts of the flesh; to teach them to clothe themselves with shame-facedness and sobriety, not with braided hair and costly apparel; and each of the young persons before us has a string of hair twisted in plaits which vanity itself might have woven: these, I repeat, must be cut off; think of the time wasted, of – "

Mr. Brocklehurst was here interrupted: three other visitors, ladies, now entered the room. They ought to have come a little sooner to have heard his lecture on dress, for they were splendidly attired in velvet, silk, and furs. The two younger of the trio (fine girls of sixteen and seventeen) had grey beaver hats, then in fashion, shaded with ostrich plumes, and from under the brim of this graceful head-dress fell a profusion of light tresses, elaborately curled; the elder lady was enveloped in a costly velvet shawl, trimmed with ermine, and she wore a false front of French curls. (1 7.32-33)

Thought: We've suspected all along that Mr. Brocklehurst was the worst kind of hypocrite, and here we get some very obvious confirmation of our suspicions. Just as he's lecturing Miss Temple on why all the girls at Lowood must have very plain clothing and hair – he's even against braids – his wife and daughters come in completely tricked out in the latest fashions with complicated hairdos and (we assume) their noses in the air. Maybe keeping the Lowood girls plain-looking is more about keeping them in their lowly place than about real Christian humility. Of course, Mr. Brocklehurst's family members aren't exactly charitable and good-hearted, either, so ironically his advice to Miss Temple does result in the girls at Lowood being, in a way, holier. But, and we might be going out on a limb here, we don't think they'd be any less holy if they were allowed to braid their hair. Just a thought.

The refreshing meal, the brilliant fire, the presence and kindness of her beloved instructress, or, perhaps, more than all these, something in her own unique mind, had roused her powers within her. They woke, they kindled: first, they glowed in the bright tint of her cheek, which till this hour I had never seen but pale and bloodless; then they shone in the liquid lustre of her eyes, which had suddenly acquired a beauty more singular than that of Miss Temple's – a beauty neither of fine colour nor long eyelash, nor pencilled brow, but of meaning, of movement, of radiance. Then her soul sat on her lips, and language flowed [...]. (1.8.51)

Thought: Helen's beauty comes, not from fancy curls or makeup, but from animation, activity, and intellectual stimulation. It's not just that "real beauty comes from the inside," although that does seem to be true in this novel – it's that Helen is at her most beautiful when she's excited about a subject that she knows a lot about and talking about it to someone she really respects. Notice that her beauty comes out most in movement and talking – it's an active rather than a passive beauty. What that means is that she's beautiful because of what she's doing, and because she's so intensely alive – not because she's a passive, static object, something to be looked at, like a beautiful painting.

I rose; I dressed myself with care: obliged to be plain – for I had no article of attire that was not made with extreme simplicity – I was still by nature solicitous to be neat. It was not my habit to be disregardful of appearance, or careless of the impression I made: on the contrary, I ever wished to look as well as I could, and to please as much as my want of beauty would permit. I sometimes regretted that I was not handsomer: I sometimes wished to have rosy cheeks, a straight nose, and small cherry mouth; I desired to be tall, stately and finely developed in figure; I felt it a misfortune that I was so little, so pale, and had features so irregular and so marked. And why had I these aspirations and these regrets? It would be difficult to say: I could not then distinctly say it to myself; yet I had a reason, and a logical, natural reason too. (1.11.47)

Thought: In this passage Jane considers appearance in several different ways. She begins by thinking about being dressed neatly and carefully – basically, not looking like a slob. But this pride in her appearance quickly turns into a lament that she isn't more of a classic beauty. She can't even admit why she wants her clothes to look nice, or to be prettier, although she claims there is a specific reason...can you guess what it might be? Yep, walks on two legs, has a deep voice, you got it.

I am sure most people would have thought him an ugly man; yet there was so much unconscious pride in his port; so much case in his demeanour; such a look of complete indifference to his own external appearance; so haughty a reliance on the power of other qualities, intrinsic or adventitious, to atone for the lack of mere personal attractiveness, that in looking at him, one inevitably shared the indifference; and even in a blind, imperfect sense, put faith in the confidence. (1.14.33)

Thought: Jane is able to separate Rochester's actual appearance from how Rochester is perceived by the people around him *and* from what she herself thinks of his character. Distinguishing appearance from personality is something she learned to do at Lowood.

And was Mr. Rochester now ugly in my eyes? No, reader: gratitude, and many associations, all pleasurable and genial, made his face the object I best liked to see; his presence in a room was more cheering than the brightest fire. Yet I had not forgotten his faults: indeed, I could not, for he brought them frequently before me. (1.15.28)

Thought: Rochester's actual appearance seems to transform as Jane's opinion of him changes (and as she starts to fall in love with him). We've got to be on the lookout with this novel for moments when someone's exterior seems to physically change – but what's *really* changing is the attitude of the person looking at them. In this passage, Jane admits that it's her feelings that make Rochester look different, but at other moments she's a little less obvious.

"Listen, then, Jane Eyre, to your sentence: to-morrow, place the glass before you, and draw in chalk your own picture, faithfully; without softening one defect: omit no harsh line, smooth away no displeasing irregularity; write under it, 'Portrait of a Governess, disconnected, poor, and plain.'

"Afterwards, take a piece of smooth ivory – you have one prepared in your drawing-box: take your pallette, mix your freshest, finest, clearest tints; choose your most delicate camel-hair pencils; delineate carefully the loveliest face you can imagine; paint it in your softest shades and sweetest hues, according to the description given by Mrs. Fairfax of Blanche Ingram: remember the raven ringlets, the oriental eye; – what! you revert to Mr. Rochester as a model! Order! No snivel! – no sentiment! – no regret! I will endure only sense and resolution. Recall the august yet harmonious lineaments, the Grecian neck and bust: let the round and dazzling arm be visible, and the delicate hand; omit neither diamond ring nor gold bracelet; portray faithfully the attire, aërial lace and glistening satin, graceful scarf and golden rose: call it 'Blanche, an accomplished lady of rank.'

"Whenever, in future, you should chance to fancy Mr. Rochester thinks well of you, take out these two picture and compare them: say, 'Mr. Rochester might probably win that noble lady's love, if he chose to strive for it; is it likely he would waste a serious thought on this indigent and insignificant plebeian?'" (2.1.72-74)

Thought: Notice that the portrait Jane draws of Blanche is completely imaginary; she hasn't seen or met Blanche yet, although we already know that Jane's drawings and paintings sometimes have an eerie way of looking just like real places and people that she's never seen. These portraits probably tell us more about the contrast between who Jane is and who she wishes she could be than about the real contrast between Jane and Blanche. It's like feeling a bit depressed, having low self-esteem, and comparing yourself to airbrushed pictures of Lindsey Lohan and Mylie Cyrus.

"Oh, sir! – never mind jewels! I don't like to hear them spoken of. Jewels for Jane Eyre sounds unnatural and strange: I would rather not have them."

"I will myself put the diamond chain round your neck, and the circlet on your forehead, – which it will become: for nature, at least, has stamped her patent of nobility on this brow, Jane; and I will clasp the bracelets on these fine wrists, and load these fairy-like fingers with rings."

"No, no, sir! think of other subjects, and speak of other things, and in another strain. Don't address me as if I were a beauty; I am your plain, Quakerish governess."

"You are a beauty in my eyes, and a beauty just after the desire of my heart, – delicate and aërial."

"Puny and insignificant, you mean. You are dreaming, sir, – or you are sneering. For God's sake don't be ironical!" (2.9.19-23)

Thought: Famous passage alert: Jane's self-description as a "plain, Quakerish governess" is one of the most important and most frequently quoted lines in the novel. Her insistence that this plain exterior is an expression of who she really is, and that jewels and fancy gowns aren't right for her, is interesting on a lot of levels. Is this just Jane's low self-esteem cropping up again? Or is it a moral stance – Jane's way of telling Rochester that she's not his mistress and that she's going to look respectable, not all tarted up with his finery? How do we read this moment knowing that another person who insisted on plainness at all cost – Mr. Brocklehurst – was a complete hypocrite? Surely Jane's not a hypocrite? So when is it OK to insist on being dressed humbly and modestly, and when is it over-acting?

His form was of the same strong and stalwart contour as ever: his port was still erect, his hair was still raven-black; nor were his features altered or sunk: not in one year's space, by any sorrow, could his athletic strength be quelled, or his vigorous prime blighted. But in his countenance, I saw a change: that looked desperate and brooding – that reminded me of some wronged and fettered wild beast or bird, dangerous to approach in his sullen woe. The caged eagle, whose gold-ringed eyes cruelty has extinguished, might look as looked that sightless Samson. (3.11.9)

Thought: English teachers are always going on about how characters change – you know, what do they learn, how do they grow, that kind of thing. Rochester's change is personal and emotional, of course, but it's also physical; you can see in his face that he really understands his (attempted) crime – and also that he's pretty much lost all hope. Being able to read information in people's faces accurately just by looking at them is something that happens a lot in this novel (and that depends on a nineteenth-century pseudo-science called "phrenology" – think of it as a palm-reading for your forehead). For more on the reference to Samson, check out the "Shout Outs" section.

Society and Class Quotes

Bessie answered not; but ere long, addressing me, she said, –

"You ought to be aware, Miss, that you are under obligations to Mrs. Reed: she keeps you: if she were to turn you off, you would have to go to the poor-house."

I had nothing to say to these words: they were not new to me: my very first recollections of existence included hints of the same kind. This reproach of my dependence had become a vague sing-song in my ear; very painful and crushing, but only half intelligible. (1.2.14-16)

Thought: Jane's early life includes constant reminders that she's poor, that she's alone, and that even her aunt and cousins consider her lower-class than they are because she won't inherit any money. Thinking of herself as beneath others, even those in the same household with her, is a habit that she learns from the very beginning.

Poverty looks grim to grown people; still more so to children: they have not much idea of industrious, working, respectable poverty; they think of the world only as connected with ragged clothes, scanty food, fireless grates, rude manners, and debasing vices: poverty for me was synonymous with degradation. (1.3.63)

Thought: Jane would refuse to live with poor relatives, even if she had any and they were loving, because the Reeds have taught her that poverty is always accompanied by immorality and unpleasantness. It's going to take Jane some time to realize that wealthy people can easily be just as degraded as poor ones – or more so.

"A new servitude! There is something in that," I soliloquized (mentally, be it understood; I did not talk aloud). "I know there is, because it does not sound too sweet; it is not like such words as Liberty, Excitement, Enjoyment: delightful sounds truly; but no more than sounds for me; and so hollow and fleeting that it is mere waste of time to listen to them. But Servitude! That must be matter of fact. Any one may serve: I have served here eight years; now all I want is to serve elsewhere." (1.10.13)

Thought: Jane's keeping it real here: she knows that she can't just up and leave Lowood and be the Queen of England tomorrow. (Besides, that job is taken, and Victoria's not going *anywhere*.) Instead of wanting complete freedom from all responsibilities, she just wants new responsibilities. She's accepted that she's just a peon, and all she's asking is a change of scenery. So her new job really isn't any kind of class or status change – just a transfer.

"I am so glad you are come; it will quite pleasant living here now with a companion. To be sure it is pleasant at any time; for Thornfield is a fine old hall, rather neglected of late years perhaps, but still it is a respectable place; yet you know in winter time, one feels dreary quite alone, in the best quarters. I say alone – Leah is a nice girl to be sure, and John and his wife are very decent people; but then you see they are only servants, and one can't converse with them on terms of equality: one must keep them at due distance, for fear of losing one's authority." (1.11.42)

Thought: Mrs. Fairfax is glad to have Jane at Thornfield because they'll be able to socialize together. Later in this chapter, we'll learn that Mrs. Fairfax is the housekeeper and household manager for Thornfield; as such she is above the regular servants, but below the master of the house, and there's hardly anyone she can talk to without compromising her position. It's a little bit like being a camp counselor: you're living with the people you're in charge of, and you can't start hanging out with them, or they won't do what you say anymore. You can only hang out with the other camp counselors.

There are people who seem to have no notion of sketching a character, or observing and describing salient points, either in persons or things: the good lady evidently belonged to this class; my queries puzzled, but did not draw her out. Mr. Rochester was Mr. Rochester in her eyes; a gentleman, a landed proprietor – nothing more: she inquired and searched no further, and evidently wondered at my wish to gain a more definite notion of his identity. (1.11.102)

Thought: Jane is frustrated that Mrs. Fairfax can only tell her Mr. Rochester's station in life instead of what kind of person he actually is. In fact, Mrs. Fairfax – like *some* people we could name – can't tell the difference between status and character, and assumes that describing him as "a gentleman" is enough. But Jane has met gentlemen like Mr. Brocklehurst, and she knows that the fact that he owns land and a house and keeps servants doesn't really tell her anything about what kind of person Rochester is. She'll have to figure that out on her own.

"The fact is, once for all, I don't wish to treat you like an inferior: that is (correcting himself), I claim only such superiority as must result from twenty years' difference in age and a century's advance in experience."

[...]

"I don't think, sir, you have a right to command me, merely because you are older than I, or because you have seen more of the world than I have – your claim to superiority depends on the use you have made of your time and experience." (1.14.42, 48)

Thought: Try *that* one on a teacher (or parent, or boss) next time they tell you they know better just because they're older and have more experience than you do.

"You have nothing to do with the master of Thornfield, further than to receive the salary he gives you for teaching his protégée, and to be grateful for such respectful and kind treatment as, if you do your duty, you have a right to expect at his hands. Be sure that is the only tie he seriously acknowledges between you and him: so don't make him the object of your fine feelings, your raptures, agonies, and so forth. He is not of your order: keep to your caste; and be too self-respecting to lavish the love of the whole heart, soul, and strength, where such a gift is not wanted and would be despised." (2.2.2)

Thought: Here Jane's trying to sort out her relationship to Rochester, and it's a lot harder because she's developed several different relationships to him that aren't entirely compatible. She's reminding herself that (1) she's his employee, (2) she's lower-class than he is, and (3) he hasn't necessarily shown a serious romantic interest in her. But that highly rational assessment really doesn't cover the instant connection they made in the forest on their first meeting, when he leaned on her shoulder to limp back to his horse and she began taking care of him.

"You should hear mama on the chapter of governesses: Mary and I have had, I should think, a dozen at least in our day; half of them detestable and the rest ridiculous, and all incubi – were they not, mama?"

"Did you speak, my own?"

The young lady thus claimed as the dowager's special property, reiterated her question with an explanation.

"My dearest, don't mention governesses; the word makes me nervous. I have suffered a martyrdom from their incompetency and caprice; I thank Heaven I have now done with them!"

Mrs. Dent here bent over to the pious lady, and whispered something in her ear; I suppose from the answer elicited, it was a reminder that one of the anathematized race was present. (2.2.97-101)

Thought: Thought #1: If Blanche Ingram were alive today she'd have been cast in that movie *Mean Girls*. Thought #2: Ranting about the lower classes right in front of them shows who's really low-class. Thought #3: Class and race seem to be getting a bit mixed up here...that's interesting. It's like someone took all their prejudices and swirled them together in a blender, and now Jane has to drink it. (Gross.)

"You are my little friend, are you not?"

"I like to serve you, sir, and to obey you in all that is right." (2.5.138-139)

Thought: You can't forget that, whatever else is going on between Jane and Rochester, they're never really equals. One of their first big conversations is an argument about whether Jane is going to let Rochester order her around and why she should, and he only wins the argument because she helps him. And remember: Jane likes to call Mr. Rochester her "master." Yeah, it's a little weird, but Jane, like Kate at the end of *The Taming of the Shrew*, knows that you can actually be in charge by seeming like you're not in charge. If you're really good at that kind of thing.

She again regarded me with a surprised stare. "I believe," she said, "I was quite mista'en in my thoughts of you: but there is so mony cheats goes about, you mun forgie me."

"And though," I continued, rather severely, "you wished to turn me from the door, on a night when you should not have shut out a dog."

"Well, it was hard: but what can a body do? I thought more o' th' childer nor of mysel: poor things! They've like nobody to tak' care on 'em but me. I'm like to look sharpish."

I maintained a grave silence for some minutes.

"You munnut think too hardly of me," she again remarked.

"But I do think hardly of you," I said; "and I'll tell you why – not so much because you refused to give me shelter, or regarded me as an impostor, as because you just now made it a species of reproach that I had no "brass", and no house. Some of the best people that ever lived have been as destitute as I am; and if you are a Christian, you ought not to consider poverty a crime." (3.3.56-61)

Thought: As a child Jane thought poverty absolutely horrible and wouldn't even consider living with poor relatives even if they were kind and hard-working people. Now, she's able to teach Hannah, from her own experience, that your moral character and your bank account (or lack of one) are completely different things.

The Supernatural Quotes

Returning, I had to cross before the looking-glass; my fascinated glance involuntarily explored the depth it revealed. All looked colder and darker in that visionary hollow than in reality: and the strange little figure there gazing at me, with a white face and arms specking the gloom, and glittering eyes of fear moving where all else was still, had the effect of a real spirit: I thought it like one of the tiny phantoms, half fairy, half imp, Bessie's evening stories represented as coming out of lone, ferny dells in moors, and appearing before the eyes of belated travelers. (1.2.24)

Thought: When Jane sees herself in the mirror as a child, she sees herself as something uncanny – perhaps a ghost or a fairy, something out of the kind of tales her nursemaid tells her by the fireside. If even Jane perceives herself as unnatural, it's not surprising that Rochester is going to be continually disconcerted by her.

Shaking my hair from my eyes, I lifted my head and tried to look boldly round the dark room: at this moment a light gleamed on the wall. Was it, I asked myself, a ray from the moon penetrating some aperture in the blind? No; moonlight was still, and this stirred; while I gazed, it glided up to the ceiling and quivered over my head. I can now conjecture readily that this streak of light was, in all likelihood, a gleam from a lantern, carried by some one across the lawn: but then, prepared as my mind was for horror, shaken as my nerves were by agitation, I thought the swift-darting beam was a herald of some coming vision from another world. My heart beat thick, my head grew hot; a sound filled my ears, which I deemed the rushing of wings: something seemed near me; I was oppressed, suffocated: endurance broke down – I uttered a wild, involuntary cry – I rushed to the door and shook the lock in a desperate effort. (1.2.32)

Thought: What actually happens to Jane during her traumatic experience in the red-room is somewhat ambiguous. The older, more experienced Jane who is narrating the story is ready to find a rational explanation for the strange light that she saw as a child; the child Jane is convinced that this light is the beginning of the manifestation of Mr. Reed's ghost. What is clear is that Jane panics before the question can be resolved – the anticipation of seeing the ghost is itself the trauma, and, as Jane will tell us, her nerves never really recover from this shock.

The laugh was repeated in its low, syllabic tone, and terminated in an odd murmur.

"Grace!" exclaimed Mrs. Fairfax.

I really did not expect any Grace to answer; for the laugh was as tragic, as preternatural a laugh as any I ever heard; and, but that it was high noon, and that no circumstances of ghostliness accompanied the curious cachination; but that neither scene nor season favoured fear, I should have been superstitiously afraid. However, the event showed me I was a fool for entertaining even a sense of surprise.

The door nearest me opened, and a servant came out, – a woman of between thirty and forty; a set, square-made figure, red-haired, and with a hard, plain face: any apparition less romantic or less ghostly could scarcely be conceived. (1.11.118-121)

Thought: Jane seems almost eager to find a ghost in the attic of Thornfield – or maybe she's just a bit paranoid because of her experience with what might have been, or seemed like, her Uncle Reed's ghost. However, her first attempt to find something creepy in the attic is unsuccessful – all she finds is a stout, middle-aged, red-headed servant. Not very eerie, that one. *Jane Eyre* the novel – and Jane Eyre the narrator – will continually tease us with things that seem spooky but turn out to be extremely plain. It's the suspense in-between the suspicion of the supernatural and the revelation of the everyday that makes the novel so exciting. Why does Jane keep looking for the supernatural? Why does the novel keep finding ways to explain away things that seem supernatural?

"No wonder you have rather the look of another world. I marvelled where you had got that sort of face. When you came upon me in Hay Lane last night, I thought unaccountably of fairy tales, and had half a mind to demand whether you had bewitched my horse: I am not sure yet. Who are your parents?"

"I have none."

"Nor ever had, I suppose: do you remember them?"

"No."

"I thought not. And so you were waiting for your people when you sat on that stile?

"For whom, sir?"

"For the men in green: it was a proper moonlight evening for them. Did I break through one of your rings, that you spread that damned ice on the causeway?"

I shook my head. "The men in green all forsook England a hundred years ago," said I, speaking as seriously as he had done. "And not even in Hay Lane or the fields about it could you find a trace of them. I don't think either summer or harvest, or winter moon, will ever shine on their revels more." (1.13.40-47)

Thought: At Jane's second meeting with Rochester, he accuses her, playfully, of being a fairy or a sprite who enchanted his horse and caused the accident in which he sprained his ankle. Jane isn't about to be outdone and banters with him readily and quick-wittedly, seeming to take fairy tales as seriously as he himself is pretending to do. Although Jane's unearthly fairy qualities are mostly a joke here, there is definitely something strange and uncanny about her quiet demeanor, plain dress, and strong personality. Rochester has met his match – and she is a little bit eerie.

Then my own thoughts worried me. What crime was this that lived incarnate in this sequestered mansion, and could neither be expelled nor subdued by the owner? – what mystery, that broke out now in fire and now in blood, at the deadest hours of night? What creature was it, that, masked in an ordinary woman's face and shape, uttered the voice, now of a mocking demon, and anon of a carrion-seeking bird of prey? (2.5.54)

Thought: Whoa, suddenly we're reading a Gothic novel! There's a secret and unnamable crime at Thornfield that can't be solved for mysterious reasons! Of course, we'll find out that it *is* a human woman – we won't call her ordinary – behind the arson and the bite wounds at Thornfield, not a demon or a vampire. The most disturbing part of the story is that this terrible crime *isn't* supernatural – just unnatural.

Presentiments are strange things! and so are sympathies; and so are signs; and the three combined make one mystery to which humanity has not yet found the key. I never laughed at presentiments in my life, because I have had strange ones of my own. Sympathies, I believe, exist (for instance, between far-distant, long-absent, wholly estranged relatives asserting, notwithstanding their alienation, the unity of the source to which each traces his origin) whose workings baffle mortal comprehension. And signs, for aught we know, may be but the sympathies of Nature with man. (2.6.1)

Thought: Foreshadowing's a strange thing too, and so is symbolism, and so are little hints from the author about supernatural tricks she'll use later to bring the main characters back together when they're dozens of miles apart. Erm, what's that called? Yeah, a *deus ex machina*. This passage is important because it's one of the only moments that Jane actually claims to the reader that she does believe in some kind of supernatural foreknowledge and also a psychic connection between people. Still, Jane suggests that these seemingly supernatural connections may have natural explanations that we just don't know about.

"I have been with my aunt, sir, who is dead."

"A true Janian reply! Good angels be my guard! She comes from the other world – from the abode of people who are dead; and tells me so when she meets me alone here in the gloaming! If I dared, I'd touch you, to see if you are substance or shadow, you elf! – but I'd as soon offer to take hold of a blue ignis fatuus light in a marsh." (2.7.21-22)

Thought: As usual Rochester is exaggerating quite a bit, but his suggestion that Jane is able to move between different worlds in a strange and uncanny way seems just about right. After all, Gateshead, Lowood, and Thornfield have practically been different *planets*. (An *ignis fatuus* or "false fire" is a little light you see in the distance when you're lost in a swamp, but it turns out to be swamp gas on fire or something like that instead of a lamp in a cottage that could lead you to safety. Ironically, later in the novel, Jane finds Moor House by following a light that she thinks is an *ignis fatuus*, but it turns out to be a lamp in a cottage.)

"It was a fairy, and come from Elf-land, it said; and its errand was to make me happy: I must go with it out of the common world to a lonely place – such as the moon, for instance – and it nodded its head towards her horn, rising over Hay-hill: it told me of the alabaster cave and silver vale where we might live. I said I should like to go; but reminded it, as you did me, that I had no wings to fly.

"'Oh,' returned the fairy, 'that does not signify! Here is a talisman will remove all difficulties;' and she held out a pretty gold ring. 'Put it,' she said, 'on the fourth finger of my left hand, and I am yours, and you are mine; and we shall leave earth, and make our own heaven yonder.' She nodded again at the moon. The ring, Adèle, is in my breeches-pocket, under the disguise of a sovereign: but I mean soon to change it to a ring again."

"But what has mademoiselle to do with it? I don't care for the fairy: you said it was mademoiselle you would take to the moon?"

"Mademoiselle is a fairy," he said, whispering mysteriously. (2.9.122-125)

Thought: Even Adèle, who is less than ten years old, thinks this fairy tale of Rochester's is ridiculous, but we think it might be just a *little* bit important that he uses a fanciful story about a magical flight to the moon as metaphors for marrying Jane. Rochester expects his marriage to Jane to be a quick fix: he'll marry her, and as soon as they've got their wedding rings on, she'll transport him into another world and all their problems will be over. Yeah, not in *this* novel, buster.

"It seemed, sir, a woman, tall and large, with thick and dark hair hanging long down her back. I know not what dress she had on: it was white and straight; but whether gown, sheet, or shroud, I cannot tell."

"Did you see her face?"

"Not at first. But presently she took my veil from its place; she held it up, gazed at it long, and then she threw it over her own head, and turned to the mirror. At that moment I saw the reflection of the visage and features quite distinctly in the dark oblong glass."

"And how were they?"

"Fearful and ghastly to me – oh, sir, I never saw a face like it! It was a discoloured face – it was a savage face. I wish I could forget the roll of the red eyes and the fearful blackened inflation of the lineaments!"

"Ghosts are usually pale, Jane."

"This, sir, was purple: the lips were swelled and dark; the brow furrowed: the black eyebrows widely raised over the bloodshot eyes. Shall I tell you of what it reminded me?"

"You may."

"Of the foul German spectre – the Vampyre." (2.10.73-81)

Thought: Is Bertha a vampire? Let's go through our Handy Vampire Checklist. Is Bertha a "blood relative" of Count Dracula? No. Does she sleep in a coffin during daylight hours? No. Is she a good candidate for villain on an episode of *Buffy the Vampire Slayer*? Maybe. Does she suck blood? Yes! Does she drain the life out of the people around her? Yes! Would a stake through the heart kill her? Yes, but it would kill you too and we're guessing you're not a vampire. So, it's complicated. (For more on this quote from a different thematic perspective, check it out in the "Foreignness and 'The Other'" section.)

All the house was still; for I believe all, except St. John and myself, were now retired to rest. The one candle was dying out: the room was full of moonlight. My heart beat fast and thick: I heard its throb. Suddenly it stood still to an inexpressible feeling that thrilled it through, and passed at once to my head and extremities. The feeling was not like an electric shock, but it was quite as sharp, as strange, as startling: it acted on my senses as if their utmost activity hitherto had been but torpor, from which they were now summoned and forced to wake. They rose expectant: eye and ear waited while the flesh quivered on my bones.

"What have you heard? What do you see?" asked St. John. I saw nothing, but I heard a voice somewhere cry –

"Jane! Jane! Jane!" – nothing more.

"O God! what is it?" I gasped.

I might have said, "Where is it?" for it did not seem in the room – nor in the house – nor in the garden; it did not come out of the air – nor from under the earth – nor from overhead. I had heard it – where, or whence, for ever impossible to know! And it was the voice of a human being – a known, loved, well-remembered voice – that of Edward Fairfax Rochester; and it spoke in pain and woe, wildly, eerily, urgently. (3.9.89-93)

Thought: If you want to impress your teacher, you should refer to this as a moment of "clairaudience," which means psychically hearing things that are far away. (Get it? Like "clairvoyance," only that's for *seeing* things that are far away.) And we'll point out again, just in case you missed it in the "What's Up With the Title?" section, that Jane's last name can be pronounced "ear," like the thing on the side of your head. So, special qualities of listening and hearing, plus an uber-special connection to Mr. Rochester, seem to make Jane clairaudient at this moment.

Morality and Ethics Quotes

"If people were always kind and obedient to those who are cruel and unjust, the wicked people would have it all their own way: they would never feel afraid, and so they would never alter, but would grow worse and worse. When we are struck at without a reason, we should strike back again very hard; I am sure we should – so hard as to teach the person who struck us never to do it again. [...] I must dislike those who, whatever I do to please them, persist in liking me; I must resist those who punish me unjustly. It is as natural as that I should love those who show me affection, or submit to punishment when I feel it is deserved." (1.6.50, 52)

Thought: Here Jane is responding to Helen Burns, who argues that you should "return good for evil," "turn the other cheek," "love your enemies," and all that sort of good Christian forgiveness stuff. Jane (remember she's only ten at this point) can't quite agree with this; she doesn't see any reason to "bless them that curse you," because then they'll get away with it! Jane's childhood ideas of justice are strict and exact – more like the Old Testament "eye for an eye" laws of retaliation than Helen's New Testament charity. It'll be interesting to see whether Jane's ideas change over time and, if so, exactly how.

"If all the world hated you, and believed you wicked, while your own conscience approved you, and absolved you from guilt, you would not be without friends."

"No: I know I should think well of myself; but that is not enough: if others don't love me, I would rather die than live – I cannot bear to be solitary and hated, Helen." (1.8.11-12)

Thought: Jane's convinced that she wouldn't be able to stick to her moral guns (so to speak) if doing so meant that she was alone and friendless. Wouldn't it be *so weird* if that was exactly what she had to learn to do by the end of the novel?

"Nature meant me to be, on the whole, a good man, Miss Eyre: one of the better end; and you see I am not so. [...] Then take my word for it, – I am not a villain: you are not to suppose that – not to attribute to me any such bad eminence; but, owing, I verily believe, rather to circumstances than to my natural bent, I am a trite common-place sinner, hackneyed in all the poor petty dissipations with which the rich and worthless try to put on life." (1.14.61)

Thought: Before Jane even really knows Rochester, he's claiming he's really not that bad a guy. We think the gentleman doth protest too much.

"Dread remorse when you are tempted to err, Miss Eyre: remorse is the poison of life."

"Repentance is said to be its cure, sir."

"It is not its cure. Reformation may be its cure; and I could reform – I have strength yet for that – if – but where is the use of thinking of it, hampered, burdened, cursed as I am? Besides, since happiness is irrevocably denied me, I have a right to get pleasure out of life: and I will get it, cost what it may." (1.14.63-65)

Thought: The difference between "repentance" and "reform" is important here. Jane thinks it's enough to repent – to feel bad for what you've done. Rochester thinks that's not enough and that you actually need to reform – to actively change your ways. We'll be watching through the rest of the novel to figure out which of them the text supports.

"You seem to doubt me; I don't doubt myself: I know what my aim is, what my motives are; and at this moment I pass a law, unalterable as that of the Medes and Persians, that both are right."

"They cannot be, sir, if they require a new statute to legalize them."

"They are, Miss Eyre, though they absolutely require a new statute: unheard-of combinations of circumstances demand unheard-of rules."

"That sounds a dangerous maxim, sir; because one can see at once that it is liable to abuse."

(1.14.83-86)

Thought: The rules say Rochester is doing something wrong, so he's out to change the rules. We don't know what the thing is that he wants to get away with, but we're suspicious already.

"I see genuine contentment in your gait and mien, your eye and face, when you are helping me and pleasing me – working for me, and with me, in, as you characteristically say, 'all that is right:' for if I bid you do what you thought wrong, there would be no light-footed running, no neat-handed alacrity, no lively glance and animated complexion. My friend would then turn to me, quiet and pale, and would say, 'No, sir; that is impossible: I cannot do it, because it is wrong;' and would become immutable as a fixed star. Well, you too have power over me, and may injure me: yet I dare not show you where I am vulnerable, lest, faithful and friendly as you are, you should transfix me at once." (2.5.140)

Thought: Later in the novel, Rochester's going to do his best to convince Jane to do something that she thinks is wrong, but notice that at this much earlier stage he already knows she's not the kind of person who can be convinced of something. Also, this passage suggests that, even though Jane kind of gets a kick out of being Rochester's servant, she won't obey just any order.

"[S]uppose you were no longer a girl well reared and disciplined, but a wild boy indulged from childhood upwards; imagine yourself in a remote foreign land; conceive that you there commit a capital error, no matter of what nature or from what motives, but one whose consequences must follow you through life and taint all your existence. Mind, I don't say a crime; I am not speaking of shedding of blood or any other guilty act, which might make the perpetrator amenable to the law: my word is error. The results of what you have done become in time to you utterly insupportable; you take measures to obtain relief: unusual measures, but neither unlawful nor culpable. Still you are miserable; for hope has quitted you on the very confines of life: your sun at noon darkens in an eclipse, which you feel will not leave it till the time of setting. Bitter and base associations have become the sole food of your memory: you wander here and there, seeking rest in exile: happiness in pleasure – I mean in heartless, sensual pleasure – such as dulls intellect and blights feeling. Heart-weary and soul-withered, you come home after years of voluntary banishment: you make a new acquaintance – how or where no matter: you find in this stranger much of the good and bright qualities which you have sought for twenty years, and never before encountered; and they are all fresh, healthy, without soil and without taint. Such society revives, regenerates: you feel better days come back – higher wishes, purer feelings; you desire to recommence your life, and to spend what remains to you of days in a way more worthy of an immortal being. To attain this end, are you justified in overleaping an obstacle of custom – a mere conventional impediment which neither your conscience sanctifies nor your judgment approves?" (2.5.148)

Thought: No matter how long and sad the story is, we can tell that Rochester's trying to trick us into saying "yes," and so can Jane. When we find out that what he's calling a "mere conventional impediment" is the law against bigamy, well, the trick's just a lot more obvious then. Still, his story does inspire a lot of sympathy.

Some time in the afternoon I raised my head, and looking round and seeing the western sun gilding the sign of its decline on the wall, I asked, "What am I to do?"

But the answer my mind gave – "Leave Thornfield at once" – was so prompt, so dread, that I stopped my ears. I said I could not bear such words now. "That I am not Edward Rochester's bride is the least part of my woe," I alleged: "that I have wakened out of most glorious dreams, and found them all void and vain, is a horror I could bear and master; but that I must leave him decidedly, instantly, entirely, is intolerable. I cannot do it."

But, then, a voice within me averred that I could do it and foretold that I should do it. I wrestled with my own resolution: I wanted to be weak that I might avoid the awful passage of further suffering I saw laid out for me; and Conscience, turned tyrant, held Passion by the throat, told her tauntingly, she had yet but dipped her dainty foot in the slough, and swore that with that arm of iron he would thrust her down to unsounded depths of agony. (3.1.1-5)

Thought: Jane's moment of great ethical crisis turns (in her mind, at least) into an allegorical scene in which Conscience and Passion start brawling, and Conscience is the bully. It's interesting that Jane knows immediately and certainly what is morally right in this situation – what's difficult isn't to know what she has to do, but to make herself do it.

"Now for the hitch in Jane's character," he said at last, speaking more calmly than from his look I had expected him to speak. "The reel of silk has run smoothly enough so far; but I always knew there would come a knot and a puzzle: here it is. Now for vexation, and exasperation, and endless trouble! By God! I long to exert a fraction of Samson's strength, and break the entanglement like tow!" (3.1.38)

Thought: Rochester sure gets compared to Samson a lot – you'll really have to check out that reference in the "Shout Outs." And, as usual, Rochester is shuffling around names and labels for things in order to try and change our attitudes toward them – that "hitch in Jane's character" is actually her *morality*.

The more solitary, the more friendless, the more unsustained I am, the more I will respect myself. I will keep the law given by God; sanctioned by man. I will hold to the principles received by me when I was sane, and not mad – as I am now. Laws and principles are not for the times when there is no temptation: they are for such moments as this, when body and soul rise in mutiny against their rigour; stringent are they; inviolate they shall be. If at my individual convenience I might break them, what would be their worth? They have a worth – so I have always believed; and if I cannot believe it now, it is because I am insane – quite insane: with my veins running fire, and my heart beating faster than I can count its throbs. Preconceived opinions, foregone determinations, are all I have at this hour to stand by: there I plant my foot. (3.1.122)

Thought: When Rochester tries to claim that Jane can reject conventional morality just because she doesn't have any family around to be offended by her decision, she realizes how much more important it is to do the right thing when you *are* alone in the world.

Foreignness and 'The Other' Quotes

I was a discord in Gateshead Hall; I was like nobody there; I had nothing in harmony with Mrs. Reed or her children, or her chosen vassalage. If they did not love me, in fact, as little did I love them. They were not bound to regard with affection a thing that could not sympathize with one amongst them; a heterogeneous thing, opposed to them in temperament, in capacity, in propensities; a useless thing, incapable of serving their interest, or adding to their pleasure; a noxious thing, cherishing the germs of indignation at their treatment, of contempt of their judgment. I know that had I been a sanguine, brilliant, careless, exacting, handsome, romping child – though equally dependent and friendless – Mrs. Reed would have endured my presence more complacently; her children would have entertained for me more of the cordiality of fellow-feeling; the servants would have been less prone to make me the scape-goat of the nursery. (1.2.30)

Thought: Even at the very beginning of her life, Jane doesn't really fit in with her surroundings; she's an outsider from the start. What seems to set her apart her and made her different from her aunt's family and household is her sense of injustice and her inability to let unfairness wash over her. There also seems no possibility of compromise, of integrating a "heterogeneous thing" like Jane into an otherwise homogenous household. Those who are unlike in temperament, the novel implies, will always be incapable of living in harmony. It's important, then, to find people to live with who may be different in class, bloodline, or situation, but are the same in attitude. (Hint, hint!) We also see, in this passage, how willing – almost eager – Jane is to characterize herself as different, as distinct.

[W]e descended, Adèle wondering whether the petit coffre was at length come; for, owing to some mistake, its arrival had hitherto been delayed. She was gratified: there it stood, a little carton, on the table when we entered the dining-room. She appeared to know it by instinct.

"Ma boîte! ma boîte!" exclaimed she, running towards it.

"Yes, there is your 'boîte' at last: take it into a corner, you genuine daughter of Paris, and amuse yourself with disembowelling it," said the deep and rather sarcastic voice of Mr. Rochester, proceeding from the depths of an immense easy-chair at the fireside. "And mind," he continued, "don't bother me with any details of the anatomical process, or any notice of the condition of the entrails: let your operation be conducted in silence: tiens-toi tranquille, enfant; comprends-tu?" (1.14.3-5)

Thought: Reading *Jane Eyre*, it can be easy to overlook the novel's interest in the French while we're thinking about Bertha Mason's origin in the West Indies or St. John Rivers' desire to go on a missionary trip to India. Of course, these British colonies and their foreignness are being directly contrasted with the foreigners next door – the French. Adèle's obsession with superficial things – fancy clothes, presents, and her appearance – is stereotyped in the novel as her inherent "Frenchness" or Parisian nature. At the very end of the novel, Jane tells us what happened to Adèle: "a sound English education corrected in a great measure her French defects." So we definitely have a sense of *Jane Eyre* as a novel with a nationalist bias – Englishness is considered normal and everything else needs to conform to it.

Seated on the carpet, by the side of this basin, was seen Mr. Rochester, costumed in shawls, with a turban on his head. His dark eyes and swarthy skin and Paynim features suited the costume exactly: he looked the very model of an Eastern emir, an agent or a victim of the bowstring. Presently advanced into view Miss Ingram. She, too, was attired in oriental fashion: a crimson scarf tied sash-like round the waist: an embroidered handkerchief knotted about her temples; her beautifully-moulded arms bare, one of them upraised in the act of supporting a pitcher, poised gracefully on her head. Both her cast of form and feature, her complexion and her general air, suggested the idea of some Israelitish princess of the patriarchal days; and such was doubtless the character she intended to represent. (2.3.11)

Thought: Rochester and Blanche act out a Bible scene in their game of charades, only to make it obvious to Jane that both of them have a certain weird foreign look to them anyway that makes it easy for them to play-act a Middle Eastern scene. Making it a scene from the Bible puts it in a sort of middle ground: it's "foreign," because it's "Eastern," but it's also familiar, because it's Judaeo-Christian. It's a case of "we have seen the Other, and it is us."

He chuckled; he rubbed his hands. "Oh, it is rich to see and hear her?" he exclaimed. "Is she original? Is she piquant? I would not exchange this one little English girl for the Grand Turk's whole seraglio, gazelle-eyes, houri forms, and all!"

The Eastern allusion bit me again. "I'll not stand you an inch in the stead of a seraglio," I said; "so don't consider me an equivalent for one. If you have a fancy for anything in that line, away with you, sir, to the bazaars of Stamboul without delay, and lay out in extensive slave-purchases some of that spare cash you seem at a loss to spend satisfactorily here."

"And what will you do, Janet, while I am bargaining for so many tons of flesh and such an assortment of black eyes?"

"I'll be preparing myself to go out as a missionary to preach liberty to them that are enslaved – your harem inmates amongst the rest. I'll get admitted there, and I'll stir up mutiny; and you, three-tailed bashaw as you are, sir, shall in a trice find yourself fettered amongst our hands: nor will I, for one, consent to cut your bonds till you have signed a charter, the most liberal that despot ever yet conferred." (2.9.129-132)

Thought: It's lucky that Rochester thinks Jane is just as good as a whole seraglio (like a harem), because apparently he's a "serial monogamist"; we know he's had at least four sexual partners – Bertha, Céline, Giacinta, and Clara – and probably others, too, and that he was aiming at bigamy this time. So, even though he relies on oriental stereotypes to talk about his own horniness, Rochester the English gentleman is the real consumer of "tons of flesh." Notice

Jane's suggestion that she could be an insurrectionary missionary – maybe there's some FORESHADOWING there?

"It seemed, sir, a woman, tall and large, with thick and dark hair hanging long down her back. I know not what dress she had on: it was white and straight; but whether gown, sheet, or shroud, I cannot tell."

"Did you see her face?"

"Not at first. But presently she took my veil from its place; she held it up, gazed at it long, and then she threw it over her own head, and turned to the mirror. At that moment I saw the reflection of the visage and features quite distinctly in the dark oblong glass."

"And how were they?"

"Fearful and ghastly to me – oh, sir, I never saw a face like it! It was a discoloured face – it was a savage face. I wish I could forget the roll of the red eyes and the fearful blackened inflation of the lineaments!"

"Ghosts are usually pale, Jane."

"This, sir, was purple: the lips were swelled and dark; the brow furrowed: the black eyebrows widely raised over the bloodshot eyes. Shall I tell you of what it reminded me?"

"You may."

"Of the foul German spectre – the Vampyre." (2.10.73-81)

Thought: If we subtract Jane's ignorance and fear from this weird description, we figure out that Bertha has a dark-colored face, large lips, and black eyebrows. A little later in the novel, we learn that Bertha's mother was Creole, which means that she had a multiracial background. So Jane is using a supernatural creature, the vampire, as a metaphor to describe a woman of color. By depicting Bertha's features in monstrous, supernatural terms, Jane characterizes herself as "afraid of the batlike undead" instead of "afraid of racial difference." Yeah, *that's* the way to deal with your fear of the unknown: turn it into something from a horror movie. (For a reading of what's going on with the horror-movie stuff here, see the discussion of this same quote under "The Supernatural.")

"These were vile discoveries; but except for the treachery of concealment, I should have made them no subject of reproach to my wife, even when I found her nature wholly alien to mine, her tastes obnoxious to me, her cast of mind common, low, narrow, and singularly incapable of being led to anything higher, expanded to anything larger – when I found that I could not pass a single evening, nor even a single hour of the day with her in comfort; that kindly conversation could not be sustained between us, because whatever topic I started, immediately received from her a turn at once coarse and trite, perverse and imbecile – when I perceived that I should

never have a quiet or settled household, because no servant would bear the continued outbreaks of her violent and unreasonable temper, or the vexations of her absurd, contradictory, exacting orders – even then I restrained myself: I eschewed upbraiding, I curtailed remonstrance; I tried to devour my repentance and disgust in secret; I repressed the deep antipathy I felt." (3.1.68)

Thought: At several points Rochester seems to admit, subtly, that the real reason his marriage to Bertha failed is "irreconcilable differences": they just didn't get along. If you took this passage and substituted the word "niece" for "wife," it could easily express Mrs. Reed's attitude toward Jane when she was a child. At Gateshead, Jane was the "heterogeneous thing," the one thing that's not like the others; in Bertha and Rochester's marriage, Bertha is in the same sort of othered position.

"One night I had been awakened by her yells – (since the medical men had pronounced her mad, she had, of course, been shut up) – it was a fiery West Indian night; one of the description that frequently precede the hurricanes of those climates. Being unable to sleep in bed, I got up and opened the window. The air was like sulphur-steams – I could find no refreshment anywhere. Mosquitoes came buzzing in and hummed sullenly round the room; the sea, which I could hear from thence, rumbled dull like an earthquake – black clouds were casting up over it; the moon was setting in the waves, broad and red, like a hot cannon-ball – she threw her last bloody glance over a world quivering with the ferment of tempest. I was physically influenced by the atmosphere and scene, and my ears were filled with the curses the maniac still shrieked out; wherein she momentarily mingled my name with such a tone of demon-hate, with such language! – no professed harlot ever had a fouler vocabulary than she: though two rooms off, I heard every word – the thin partitions of the West India house opposing but slight obstruction to her wolfish cries." (3.1.75)

Thought: Aww, poor Rochester. He goes to Jamaica to get in on the whole colonial-exploitation thing, marries a woman to get rich, and he doesn't like her and she has mental problems. Now he has to deal with hot weather and mosquitoes and that pesky Bertha screaming and screaming at night because he's imprisoned her in their house. These British colonies are sure a hellish experience for the overlords using them to get rich quick.

"A wind fresh from Europe blew over the ocean and rushed through the open casement: the storm broke, streamed, thundered, blazed, and the air grew pure. I then framed and fixed a resolution. While I walked under the dripping orange-trees of my wet garden, and amongst its drenched pomegranates and pine-apples, and while the refulgent dawn of the tropics kindled round me – I reasoned thus, Jane – and now listen; for it was true Wisdom that consoled me in that hour, and showed me the right path to follow.

"The sweet wind from Europe was still whispering in the refreshed leaves, and the Atlantic was thundering in glorious liberty; my heart, dried up and scorched for a long time, swelled to the tone, and filled with living blood – my being longed for renewal – my soul thirsted for a pure draught. I saw hope revive – and felt regeneration possible. From a flowery arch at the bottom of my garden I gazed over the sea – bluer than the sky: the old world was beyond; clear

prospects opened thus: –

"'Go,' said Hope, 'and live again in Europe: there it is not known what a sullied name you bear, nor what a filthy burden is bound to you.'" (3.1.78-80)

Thought: Have you ever felt convinced that the problem wasn't you, it was the crumby place you lived? Rochester can't be to blame here; it's not like he got himself into this situation with Bertha in the West Indies. The problem must be Jamaica itself. If he goes back to Europe, everything will be good and civilized again. There's no chance that he himself was the original problem and that wherever he goes he'll take it with him.

"This parlour is not his sphere," I reflected: "the Himalayan ridge or Caffre bush, even the plague-cursed Guinea Coast swamp would suit him better. Well may he eschew the calm of domestic life; it is not his element: there his faculties stagnate – they cannot develop or appear to advantage. It is in scenes of strife and danger – where courage is proved, and energy exercised, and fortitude tasked – that he will speak and move, the leader and superior. A merry child would have the advantage of him on this hearth. He is right to choose a missionary's career – I see it now." (3.8.31)

Thought: Rochester used a British colonial outpost (Jamaica) as a get-rich-quick scheme. St. John, on the other hand, is planning to use a British colonial outpost (India) as a sort of adventure playground. Ah, the many different kinds of exploitation!

In leaving England, I should leave a loved but empty land – Mr. Rochester is not there; and if he were, what is, what can that ever be to me? [...] Of course (as St. John once said) I must seek another interest in life to replace the one lost: is not the occupation he now offers me truly the most glorious man can adopt or God assign? Is it not, by its noble cares and sublime results, the one best calculated to fill the void left by uptorn affections and demolished hopes? I believe I must say, Yes – and yet I shudder. Alas! If I join St. John, I abandon half myself: if I go to India, I go to premature death. (3.8.114)

Thought: Jane's conviction that going to India would kill her – and the novel's implication that it *does* kill St. John later – just shows the British prejudice against it. Obviously, suggests this messed up line of reasoning, a little English angel like Jane could never survive in *India*, which is, let's face it, that worst possible thing, *not English*.

The Home Quotes

Probably, if I had lately left a good home and kind parents, this would have been the hour when I should most keenly have regretted the separation: that wind would then have saddened my heart; this obscure chaos would have disturbed my peace: as it was I derived from both a strange excitement, and reckless and feverish, I wished the wind to howl more wildly, the gloom to deepen to darkness, and the confusion to rise to clamour. (1.6.14)

Thought: Jane claims that, because she came from an unpleasant home where she felt unwelcome, she is excited rather than depressed by her situation at Lowood, symbolized here by the windy chaos outside the window. We're not sure, however, if we should believe her; even though her life at Gateshead was unpleasant, any change is distressing, especially for a child, and maybe she *is* mourning for the home she had before, even if it wasn't too great. Jane's first comment on her homelessness makes us realize that she's not always a completely honest narrator, and we might have to dig deep to figure out her real feelings.

Well has Solomon said: – "Better is a dinner of herbs where love is, than a stalled ox and hatred therewith."

I would not now have exchanged Lowood with all its privations, for Gateshead and its daily luxuries. (1.8.60-61)

Thought: Despite the fact that she doesn't get enough to eat at Lowood and can be mocked and maligned by Mr. Brocklehurst, Jane prefers it to the red velvet curtains and cruelty of her Aunt Reed at Gateshead. Home, for Jane, isn't just a roof over her head; it's being accepted for who she is and having the opportunity to better herself.

On a dark, misty, raw morning in January, I had left a hostile roof with a desperate and embittered heart – a sense of outlawry and almost of reprobation – to seek the chilly harbourage of Lowood: that bourne so far away and unexplored. The same hostile roof now again rose before me: my prospects were doubtful yet; and I had yet an aching heart. I still felt as a wanderer on the face of the earth; but I experienced firmer trust in myself and my own powers, and less withering dread of oppression. The gaping wound of my wrongs, too, was now quite healed; and the flame of resentment extinguished. (2.6.114)

Thought: Returning to Gateshead after she has been at Thornfield for six months and Lowood for eight years before that, Jane doesn't have any sense of homecoming – but at least she no longer feels bitter about her childhood experience with the Reeds. She is able to see her aunt's house again without fear, even though she'll never feel like it was really a home.

How people feel when they are returning home from an absence, long or short, I did not know: I had never experienced the sensation. I had known what it was to come back to Gateshead when a child, after a long walk – to be scolded for looking cold or gloomy; and later, what it was to come back from church to Lowood – to long for a plenteous meal and a good fire, and to be unable to get either. Neither of these returnings were very pleasant or desirable: no magnet drew me to a given point, increasing in its strength of attraction the nearer I came. The return to Thornfield was yet to be tried. (2.7.8)

Thought: Jane has done plenty of going back to places, but not much actual going home. She's never felt connected to a place, which is strange because there are only three places she remembers living. Perhaps returning to Thornfield will feel different; it's possible that Jane has finally found the home she never had. It's also interesting that she thinks she'll only be able to tell what feels like home after leaving it and returning. In this novel, being away from home is the thing that makes it possible to know what home is.

"Thank you, Mr. Rochester, for your great kindness. I am strangely glad to get back again to you; and wherever you are is my home, – my only home." (2.7.34)

Thought: Given the way Jane doesn't seem to connect to places, but to people and the way they do or don't allow her to be herself, it's not surprising that her "home" is established in terms of companionship.

I skirted fields, and hedges, and lanes till after sunrise. I believe it was a lovely summer morning: I know my shoes, which I had put on when I left the house, were soon wet with dew. But I looked neither to rising sun, nor smiling sky, nor wakening nature. He who is taken out to pass through a fair scene to the scaffold, thinks not of the flowers that smile on his road, but of the block and axe-edge; of the disseverment of bone and vein; of the grave gaping at the end: and I thought of drear flight and homeless wandering – and oh! with agony I thought of what I left. (3.1.161)

Thought: Jane's most courageous moral decision takes the form of abandoning the home she has found for herself with Rochester. Her decision to become homeless means that she is physically unmoored – but ethically grounded.

I touched the heath: it was dry, and yet warm with the heat of the summer day. I looked at the sky; it was pure: a kindly star twinkled just above the chasm ridge. The dew fell, but with propitious softness; no breeze whispered. Nature seemed to me benign and good; I thought she loved me, outcast as I was; and I, who from man could anticipate only mistrust, rejection, insult, clung to her with filial fondness. To-night, at least, I would be her guest, as I was her child: my mother would lodge me without money and without price. (3.2.6)

Thought: For at least a little while, Jane returns to the home that we can find in Nature – it's almost like a garden-of-Eden thing. It also strikes us that going out onto the moors and trusting that Nature will care for you has an Israelites-in-the-wilderness feel. Jane even finds some manna – OK, berries, but close enough. Unfortunately, hunger will drive her back to "civilization" and houses.

"And what business have you here?" she continued. "It is not your place. Mary and I sit in the kitchen sometimes, because at home we like to be free, even to license – but you are a visitor, and must go into the parlour." (3.3.72)

Thought: You know how, at parties, everyone always ends up in the kitchen, even if you put all the food and drinks in the living room? That's what Jane did here – ended up in the kitchen because it seems like that's where the action is. Diana's trying to be kind by suggesting Jane go into the parlor, which implies that Jane is being treated as a high-class visitor, but actually she's just reminding Jane of her own homelessness and the way she doesn't belong at Moor House.

My home, then, when I at last find a home, – is a cottage; a little room with whitewashed walls and a sanded floor, containing four painted chairs and a table, a clock, a cupboard, with two or three plates and dishes, and a set of tea-things in delf. Above, a chamber of the same dimensions as the kitchen, with a deal bedstead and chest of drawers; small, yet too large to be filled with my scanty wardrobe: though the kindness of my gentle and generous friends has increased that, by a modest stock of such things as are necessary. (3.5.1)

Thought:: This is the first (and only) time in *Jane Eyre* that Jane actually has a little house all to herself that she can call home, and it won't last very long.

"You think so now," rejoined St. John, "because you do not know what it is to possess, nor consequently to enjoy wealth: you cannot form a notion of the importance twenty thousand pounds would give you; of the place it would enable you to take in society; of the prospects it would open to you: you cannot – '

"And you," I interrupted, "cannot at all imagine the craving I have for fraternal and sisterly love. I never had a home, I never had brothers or sisters; I must and will have them now: you are not reluctant to admit me and own me, are you?" (3.7.127)

Thought: So what would you do if you won the lottery? Move into a small house with three of your cousins so that you had somewhere to call home? Yeah, we didn't think so. But that's what Jane wants to do.

Plot Analysis

Classic Plot Analysis

Initial Situation

Jane is a poor orphan girl with nothing to help her in the world but a few nasty relatives and her education as a teacher of music, drawing, and French. OK, actually, it's only the education that will help her – and her own initiative.

Explanation/Discussion: Notice that this "initial situation" is a long time developing in this novel. We've skipped right through Jane's experiences at Gateshead with the Reeds and at Lowood with Mr. Brocklehurst, and the real beginning of the main plot is the moment when Jane goes out into the world on her own to seek her fortune. If you wanted to, you could probably diagram Jane's childhood experiences as their own story – they're like little plotlets, episodes that happen before the most important action in the novel gets going. That doesn't mean that Jane's childhood isn't interesting; after all, Jane develops the most as a character during her formative years, and the rest of the novel is really about how she reacts to the world once she's been formed.

Conflict

Jane falls in love with her new employer, Mr. Rochester, but can't act on her feelings because they are separated by rank and fortune.

Well, really, there are lots of reasons she feels she can't act on her feelings: she doesn't want to seem like she has ideas above her station, and Rochester is pretending to be interested in this nasty hussy Blanche Ingram. It might be difficult to see Jane's unattainable desire to be Rochester's wife as the central conflict here, but don't worry – there are a lot of different conflicts here at the center of the novel. Despite the side-conflicts between Jane and Mr. Brocklehurst or Jane and Mrs. Reed, the real conflict here is between Jane and the world – Jane and circumstances. She's separated from Rochester by money and status, but also by logistics, awkward situations, Rochester's own teasing, and lots more. It's Jane against all the things that are keeping her from being with the man she loves.

Complication

It turns out that Mr. Rochester is married already – to a madwoman!

It's one heck of a complication, isn't it? The revelation that Mr. Rochester's wife is alive, living in the attic, and homicidal – and that he's legally prevented from divorcing her because she's been diagnosed as insane – seems like it will sunder Jane and Rochester forever. It also sets up one of the most important foil relationships of the novel – Bertha Mason, "the madwoman in the attic," as a foil to Jane herself. (See the "Character Analysis" section on Bertha Mason for more on this.)

Climax

Jane runs away from Thornfield so that she won't be tempted to live in sin with Rochester.

It's somewhat ironic that the climactic moment of the novel is one in which the lovers part, seemingly never to be reunited. We can tell that this is the climax because we're faced with an either-or choice for what will happen next. From here, either Jane will go back to Thornfield and be reconciled with Rochester, or she'll strike out into the world and never see him again – those are pretty much the only options.

Suspense

Jane considers going to India with St. John Rivers to do missionary work.

This is the "suspense" part because we're holding our breath. Is Jane going to go with St. John because she feels she needs to devote herself to some grand cause? Is she going to marry St. John just because he keeps pestering her to give in? Will Rochester rescue her before she makes a mistake that could last for the rest of her life? Or, knowing Jane, will she come to her senses and

Denouement

Jane mysteriously hears Mr. Rochester's voice from miles away and feels called back to him.

We breathe a sigh of relief. Whether this is actually a supernatural moment of clairaudience, where Jane really does hear Rochester from miles away through their sympathetic connection, or whether it's just a delusion that Jane's brain invents to keep her from agreeing to marry St. John, we know it's going to be alright now. Jane's going to go back to Thornfield and find out where Rochester is, and she's never going to leave him again.

Conclusion

Jane and Rochester get married and live happily ever after (even though Rochester is minus one eye and one hand). It's implied that St. John Rivers dies alone in India.

Well, that's pretty much all there is to it: a wedding and a death are pretty good signs that this is the conclusion of the novel. You might want to check out "What's Up With the Ending?" to get our thoughts on why St. John Rivers is the last character mentioned in the book.

Booker's Seven Basic Plots Analysis: Rags to Riches

Initial wretchedness at home and the 'Call'

After a horrible childhood living with her aunt and cousins, Jane gets some solid education at Lowood Institute and becomes a teacher.

Jane starts out, living at Gateshead Hall, as the lowest of the low, hated by her aunt, tormented by her cousins – heck, even the servants put her in her place on a regular basis. Worst of all, crime and punishment seem backwards here – John Reed gets rewarded for bullying Jane, and she gets punished for defending herself. Jane's traumatic experience in the "red-room" acts as her "call" into the wider world – it draws the attention of a powerful man like Mr. Lloyd, who is able to make arrangements for her to go away to school, where she can actually gain skills and make something of herself away from the malevolent influence of Mrs. Reed.

Out into the world, initial success

Jane gets wanderlust, advertises her services as a governess, gets a position at Thornfield, and everything seems to be going swimmingly – especially when she gets engaged to her employer, Mr. Rochester.

Notice that Jane goes "out into the world" twice – first, she moves from Gateshead to Lowood, and then from Lowood to Thornfield. Baby steps. What do you think the novel might gain from doubling up this part of the plot? As for the success, that happens not just twice but three times. First, after Jane proves herself honest at Lowood, she's able to concentrate on studying and become a teacher. Then, after she proves herself resourceful, she gets a job at Thornfield. We sort of assume that Jane is a good governess (Rochester says so at least once) even though we don't really hear a lot about her teaching. Last but not least is Jane's matrimonial success – her engagement to Mr. Rochester.

The central crisis

Jane is faced with a choice: make an ethical exception and live in sin with Rochester because maybe it's not really sin, or stick to her guns and turn her back on temptation.

This is the really murky moment, where we know that Jane is doing the right thing, but we *almost* think that she should just stay with Rochester and pretend to be married to him, because we can tell they're meant to be together. The tragic thing is that Jane can also tell they're made for each other – but she knows that she can't let Rochester commit bigamy, or be a part of it. For a little bit here, it looks like Jane will have to choose between happiness and morality. Her choice may be right, but it leaves both of them miserable.

Independence and the final ordeal

Rather than subjecting herself to being Rochester's mistress, Jane strikes out on her own and becomes a village school-mistress. Things seem OK, if not great, until she has to contend with romantic pressure from her cousin St. John Rivers.

A lot of important stuff happens here. Jane proves that she doesn't need Rochester to make it in the world – even going door to door, begging for food and shelter, Jane is able to find somewhere to live, find a job, and earn her keep. As if that's not enough, she inherits a little money, making her financially independent for the long term. But these proofs of her own strength come along with her new battle against St. John Rivers – basically, a battle for control of her soul, which she almost loses.

Final union, completion, and fulfillment

Jane is mysteriously called back to Rochester when she hears his voice from miles away. Although he has lost a hand and an eye, and his remaining eye is blind, they marry. After two years, his sight gradually returns, and they live in "perfect concord."

Explanation/Discussion: It's a storybook happy ending; Princess Charming (Jane) has come back to the now-ruined castle (Thornfield) to rescue the Prince from his melancholy, lonely life. He even miraculously gets his sight back...in the one eye, at least. Clairaudience, reunions, weddings, un-blindings – it's practically a grab-bag of miracles. (Meanwhile, the Other Guy, St. John, went to India as a missionary and has basically worked himself to death, but, erm, that had to happen, didn't it?)

Three Act Plot Analysis

Act I

After a thorough but somewhat lonely education at Lowood Institute, Jane becomes the governess at Thornfield and quickly falls in love with her master, Mr. Edward Rochester.

Act II

Jane and Rochester try to get married, but they're prevented because Rochester is trying to commit bigamy – he already has a wife locked in a room on the third floor at Thornfield. Jane runs away.

Act III

Jane learns that marriage without passion would be immoral when she's faced with a proposal from her clergyman cousin, St. John Rivers. She returns to Rochester, who has conveniently become a widow while she was gone, and they marry.

Study Questions

1. How would this novel be different if it was titled *The Governess*? If it was titled *Redemption* ? If it was titled (to steal from Gilbert and Gubar) *The Madwoman in the Attic*? (See "Brain

Snacks" for a discussion of Gilbert and Gubar.)
2. What would happen to the story if Jane were beautiful instead of plain? Would it matter?
3. If Jane and Rochester are "akin," then what is their "kind"? What do they actually share, and what made them similar in the first place?
4. *Jane Eyre* is divided into three books and also takes place in three (OK, maybe four) main settings: Gateshead and Lowood (childhood), Thornfield (young love), Moor House/Morton (temporary banishment). But the books don't match up exactly with the three main sections of the plot. Why does the novel break after Book I, Chapter 15 (Jane saves Rochester from burning to death in his bed) and again after Book II, Chapter 11 (Jane discovers Rochester's attempt at bigamy)? What might the events of these two chapters have in common?
5. Is there anything supernatural in *Jane Eyre* that doesn't get explained away? If so, what?
6. Does the reader feel sorry for Bertha Mason? Does Rochester treat her fairly? Does she seem as bad as he suggests?
7. Is Jane's ethical sense innate? Is she born knowing right from wrong, or does she learn the difference?
8. Do you always agree with Jane's decision to stand on principle, or are there ways that the novel makes us wish she were a little more flexible? (Hint: think about the characters who argue with Jane about ethics, especially Helen Burns, St. John Rivers, and Mr. Rochester.)
9. Why does Rochester like to describe Jane as some kind of supernatural creature – an elf, a fairy, a sprite, etc.? Does she have an "elfin" feel to the reader, or is he just making fun of her?
10. How does *Jane Eyre* set up the relationship between England and different foreign places – the West Indies, including Jamaica; France and the European Continent; and an orientalized version of Asia? What influences seem to come from each of these places, and how do they get stereotyped? How should the contemporary reader respond to these stereotypes?

Characters

All Characters

Jane Eyre Character Analysis

If Jane had her way, she would probably tell us that she doesn't have any character to speak of; she's happy just to be Mr. Rochester's "plain, Quakerish governess," an orphan-turned-teacher whose clothes are all either black or gray and who never really kicks the habit of calling Rochester her "master." Jane spends a lot of time as a wallflower trying to fade into the woodwork – sometimes literally, such as at the moment where she hides in the shadows at the end of the hall while Blanche Ingram and a group of dolled-up ladies sweep past. She even tries to hide herself in the story she's telling; we've figured out that she's in love with Rochester long before she actually tells us. But somehow we get the idea that, her reticence and meekness aside, Jane is actually one of the strongest and most intense characters in the novel.

Get Dr. Spock on the Line

It all starts with Jane's childhood trauma in the "red-room," a weird bedroom at Gateshead where her Uncle Reed died nine years before. When Jane stands up to her nasty cousin John Reed, her aunt locks her in the red-room alone as a punishment – it's just Jane, a lot of red velvet furnishings, a few white things, and an eerie silence. Then something starts happening – maybe it's the ghost appearing, maybe not, but Jane completely loses it. We talk about the symbolism of the red-room itself under "Symbols, Imagery, Allegory," and you can read more about it there, but let's think about the effect of this experience on Jane's character, and what it means that she had the experience in the first place. (Try to forget for a minute that she's ten years old at this point, which seems a little old to us to be afraid of ghosts or antique furniture.) Here's how Jane describes her feelings while she's locked in the red-room:

What a consternation of soul was mine that dreary afternoon! How all my brain was in tumult, and all my heart in insurrection! Yet in what darkness, what dense ignorance, was the mental battle fought! I could not answer the ceaseless inward question – why I thus suffered; now, at the distance of – I will not say how many years, I see it clearly. (1.2.29)

What we get from this is that Jane is "in her own head" a lot, always analyzing everything that happens to her and trying to figure out why it's happening that way. She doesn't just object to being locked in the red-room because it isn't decorated up to Martha Stewart's exacting standards or because the red curtains give it bad *feng shui*. What she objects to is being imprisoned for behaving in self-defense, because that's not fair. It's not the punishment itself that's the real problem in her mind – just the fact that she *is* being punished without good cause. In this interpretation, the red-room is just an innocent bystander – Jane's trauma there is the "mental battle" that children have to go through at some point to recognize that there is unchallenged injustice in the world, and some of it might happen to them personally. With that said, it doesn't seem like a blue room or an animal-print-themed room would have quite the same significance here.

Hitting Your Desk With A Ruler Always Gets Their Attention

Jane will go through a lot of different relationships over the years, but most of them boil down to one basic dynamic: the teacher-student connection. Jane's ticket out of Gateshead is agreeing to become a student at Lowood Institute, and she finally gains the approval of the people around her for the first time in her life by working hard and making herself into a *good* student. Her study skills make it possible for her to become a teacher and a governess – in other words, to have a career and earn a living, which was a difficult thing for a woman, especially a young, single woman with no powerful friends, to do in Victorian England.

So far, so good, right? But here's the thing: the fact that teacher-student relationships are central to Jane's success means that she often has trouble letting them go. In fact, the way she relates to most of the people in her life, from Helen Burns to Diana and St. John Rivers to Mr. Rochester himself, is either as their master or their pupil (or sometimes both).

This starts with Helen; she's close to Jane's age and Jane's first real friend, but she also knows a lot more than Jane does – both about schoolwork and about Christian morality. She's not Jane's equal, she's Jane's teacher, or at least someone that Jane hero-worships and learns from. Jane's cousin Diana Rivers will be a very similar type of friend; Jane tells us directly that, when she's hanging out with Diana and Mary, "If in our trio there was a superior and a leader, it was Diana" (3.4.4). According to Jane, this is because "the part of instructress pleased and suited her" and "that of scholar pleased and suited me no less" (3.4.4). In relation to her female friends, then, Jane often reverts to the dynamic she learned as a child, where she is the faithful pupil and the compassionate women around her are her teachers.

The men in Jane's life are a somewhat different story. Jane doesn't naturally look up to them as friendly teachers, perhaps simply because all of her formative experiences at Lowood involved authority figures who were either intelligent, loving women or selfish, hypocritical men. This makes it tough for Jane to relate to men like Rochester or St. John, because she doesn't have a pre-set emotional pattern for dealing with men who aren't trying to cut off the hair of orphan girls to make them humble or some other weird thing like that. When Jane and Rochester argue about their relationship, for example, Jane won't let Rochester claim that he's older and therefore wiser; she'll call him "master" and take his orders to humor him because he's her employer, but she knows that he's not always right, and she doesn't hesitate to lecture him if she thinks that, at a particular moment, she needs to be his governess, too, as well as Adèle's.

Finally, there's St. John Rivers. At first, Jane is able to stand up to St. John, look him in the eye, and tell him exactly what she does and doesn't need in her life. But once she agrees to let St. John teach her Hindustani, she seems to be more and more under his thumb all the time:

I found him a very patient, very forbearing, and yet an exacting master: he expected me to do a great deal; and when I fulfilled his expectations, he, in his own way, fully testified his approbation. By degrees, he acquired a certain influence over me that took away my liberty of mind: his praise and notice were more restraining than his indifference. I could no longer talk or laugh freely when he was by, because a tiresomely importunate instinct reminded me that vivacity (at least in me) was distasteful to him. I was so fully aware that only serious moods and occupations were acceptable, that in his presence every effort to sustain or follow any other became vain: I fell under a freezing spell. When he said "go," I went; "come," I came; "do this," I did it. But I did not love my servitude: I wished, many a time, he had continued to neglect me. (3.8.68)

Becoming St. John's student and obeying him the way she would obey a teacher makes it difficult for Jane to maintain her own personality and nature. She won't ever really break away from St. John's influence under her own power, and she'll only be able to go back to Rochester when St. John leaves to visit Cambridge for a few weeks and she stops feeling like his pupil.

But I AM holier than thou!

For the first ten years of Jane's life, she is bullied and teased and lorded over and sometimes even beaten. But then the really interesting thing happens: without any support, without any friend or mentor or teacher (except Bessie, the nursemaid, who is *sometimes* a *little bit* nice to her), she rises up against oppression. This is only the first of many times that Jane's going to show a keen ethical sensibility that seems to come out of nowhere. Without any teaching, without anyone else to validate her, Jane knows what's right and what's wrong, and it makes her furious when people get away with injustice.

While she's at Lowood, Jane's encounter with Helen Burns teaches her about a different kind of reaction to suffering and injustice – a New Testament "love your enemies," "turn the other cheek" philosophy. For Helen, what's right is not to insist on your own rights, but to be continually meek and forgiving and emulate Jesus. Jane is amazed by this attitude, but she's not able to adopt it:

"I feel this, Helen; I must dislike those who, whatever I do to please them, persist in disliking me; I must resist those who punish me unjustly. It is as natural as that I should love those who show me affection, or submit to punishment when I feel it is deserved." (1.6.52)

So Jane, at least at first, is one of those people who can't let anything go by – she has to stand up for herself and for a strict interpretation of moral laws. If Helen Burns represents New Testament love and forgiveness at this point, the child version of Jane Eyre represents an Old Testament code of justice as retaliation – "an eye for an eye" stuff. (Technically this is called the *lex talionis*, which means "the law of the claw" – cool, eh? – although that phrase doesn't get used in the novel.) You can probably guess what this means for the plot – Jane's going to have to learn when to stand on principle, when to forgive, and how to tell the difference between those situations.

Jane's big ethical crisis as an adult is her reaction to Rochester's attempt to make her his mistress. Her decision to abandon the man she loves, who is offering her affection, money, and an easy life, shows once again what a strong sense of principle she has. In fact, at this point, we find her clinging to principle just a little bit irritating. Couldn't she cut Rochester a break? He's really in a bind, and he does love her. Maybe that's why she needs to meet St. John Rivers and learn why hard work and ethics are great, but they don't exactly keep you warm at night, if you know what we mean. Jane's decision to go back to Rochester and let him know that she's forgiven him comes when she supernaturally hears his voice out of nowhere – not when she finds out that he's become a widow. Maybe her principles *do* change toward the end of the novel; maybe she learned something from Helen Burns after all.

<u>It's a bird! It's a plane! It's...an elf?</u>

So far, we've suggested that Jane is famous for her plainness (plain Jane . . . get it?) and her morality. That sounds just great, right? But maybe not very interesting? Well, here's the thing: Jane is also just a little bit weird. A little eerie. A little...otherworldly. We're not going to go so far as to say that she's actually a fairy or an elf, but there are a lot of moments where she seems a bit strange: when she looks into the mirror as a child, for example, she doesn't recognize herself. When Rochester meets her, she spooks his horse. Her moods change quickly and she's always bantering with Rochester or being sweetly contrary. It's no wonder that Rochester thinks she's some kind of malicious sprite:

"When you came on me in Hay Lane last night, I thought unaccountably of fairy tales, and had half a mind to demand whether you had bewitched my horse: I am not sure yet." (1.13.40)

"If I dared, I'd touch you, to see if you are substance or shadow, you elf! – but I'd as soon offer to take hold of a blue ignis fatuus *light in a marsh."* (2.7.22)

"You mocking changeling – fairy-born and human-bred! You make me feel as I have not felt these twelve months." (3.11.106)

Why is Jane always being compared, especially by Rochester, to these supernatural creatures? Well, she may not actually be a fairy, but let's think about what she does have that seems unusual or unnatural or different from everyone else:

- She's definitely an outsider; she can make friends, but nobody seems like her – she's a special unique individual. (Aww.)
- She's not willing to accept that Rochester is her superior just because he's an older, more experienced man; that's definitely an unusual level of pluck for a Victorian heroine.
- She's unmoored; she doesn't really have a home or a real family of her own, so she seems to have been dropped into the world without any connections from some mysterious other place.
- Most importantly, she's the first woman who's ever told Rochester "no." And we're not just talking about, "no, Mr. Rochester, I don't want you to buy me any fancy dresses, thanks." We're talking about the big N-O, the one they're always reminding you is an option in your sex ed class. Rochester may have had Bertha, he may have had Céline and Giacinta and Clara, but he's not going to have Jane until she's good and ready and she thinks it's morally OK.

All these different kinds of unusual resistance, strength, and integrity make Jane practically a space alien in the world of the novel, so it's no wonder that Rochester's always characterizing her as a fairy or elf or otherworldly spirit.

<u>What's in a name?</u>

Then there's the problem of Jane's last name, how to pronounce it, and what it means – but we've covered that in the "What's Up With the Title?" and "Character Clues" sections, so you should check it out there.

Jane Eyre Timeline and Summary

- Jane is living with her Aunt Reed and cousins at Gateshead, being bullied and tormented by John Reed in particular.
- Jane finally can't take it anymore and fights back against John.
- Jane is locked in the "red-room," the bedchamber in which her uncle died, as a punishment, and has a traumatic, eerie experience.
- Jane is sent to Lowood Institute, a religious school for orphan girls.
- Jane studies hard and eventually becomes a teacher at Lowood.

- Jane gets a spot of wanderlust and applies to be a governess.
- Jane gets a job at Thornfield as the governess to a little French girl named Adèle Varens.
- Jane meets the master of Thornfield, Mr. Rochester, and quickly falls in love with him.
- Jane has a series of eerie experiences related to a mysterious locked room on the third floor of Thornfield and a creepy woman's laugh that she hears coming from behind the door.
- Mr. Rochester teases Jane by pretending to be interested in a local debutante, Blanche Ingram.
- Jane goes back to Gateshead to tend Mrs. Reed on her deathbed.
- Jane returns to Thornfield and eventually becomes engaged to Mr. Rochester.
- Jane and Rochester's wedding is interrupted by two men who reveal that Rochester is already married.
- Jane leaves Thornfield and wanders alone on the moors, friendless and starving.
- Arriving at Moor House, Jane is taken in by Diana, Mary, and St. John Rivers.
- After regaining her strength, with St. John's help, Jane gets a job as a teacher in a village school in Morton and moves to her own cottage.
- Jane discovers that she and the Rivers siblings are cousins and that she has inherited £20,000.
- St. John Rivers asks Jane to marry him and go with him to India on a missionary trip.
- Jane mysteriously hears Rochester calling her from a great distance.
- Jane returns to Thornfield and marries Mr. Rochester.
- Jane and Rochester have a son.

Mr. Rochester Character Analysis

Mr. Rochester is stern-featured, heavy-browed, craggy-faced, rude, abrupt, horny, twice Jane's age, always on the edge of violence, likes to order people around, keeps his wife locked in the attic, and teases Jane on at least one occasion until she cries. Here's the crazy part: *that's why he's so awesome.* He may be fantastically ugly. He may be kind of a jerk. But he's real! Well, OK, he's not real. He's a character in *Jane Eyre.* But you know what we're talking about; he's a genuine-seeming character, not some stuck-up, pompous, handsome young man who smoothly says all the right things and doesn't have any personality of his own. That's why this is not a Jane Austen novel – those are great, too, but this novel isn't about proper behavior; it's about *passion.*

Tales as old as time

Rochester is sort of like the Beast half of a "Beauty and the Beast" story. (Forget for a minute that Jane's no beauty.) He's even got a sort of shaggy mane of hair that makes him look beast-ish, and at the end of the novel, when he's locked himself away at Ferndean to wallow in his own self-pity, he's described as "some wronged and fettered wild beast or bird, dangerous to approach in his sullen woe" (3.11.9). Of course, if Rochester is the Beast, then Jane will have to do something to tame him. Instead of subduing him once and for all, she develops little ways of manipulating him – making him irritated when he's horny so that he curses her instead of hitting on her, for example, when they're engaged for the first time:

In other people's presence I was, as formerly, deferential and quiet; any other line of conduct being uncalled for: it was only in the evening conferences I thus thwarted and afflicted him. He continued to send for me punctually the moment the clock struck seven; though when I appeared before him now, he had no such honeyed terms as "love" and "darling" on his lips: the best words at my service were "provoking puppet," "malicious elf," "sprite," "changeling," &c. For caresses, too, I now got grimaces; for a pressure of the hand, a pinch on the arm; for a kiss on the cheek, a severe tweak of the ear. It was all right: at present I decidedly preferred these fierce favours to anything more tender. […] Meantime, Mr. Rochester affirmed I was wearing him to skin and bone, and threatened awful vengeance for my present conduct at some period fast coming. I laughed in my sleeve at his menaces. "I can keep you in reasonable check now," I reflected; "and I don't doubt to be able to do it hereafter: if one expedient loses its virtue, another must be devised."

Yet after all my task was not an easy one; often I would rather have pleased than teased him. (2.9.171-172)

There's more danger than anything else in these strange evening dates. At points the reader is just a little bit nervous that Rochester's a bit too wild or a bit too incapable of restraining his desires. We're admittedly a little afraid for what might happen to Jane at some of those moments when he wildly clasps her to him. Perhaps that's one reason Rochester gets compared in the novel to Bluebeard, the mythical nobleman who gets into a marry-and-murder cycle with one wife after another. There's also a hint of the *Arabian Nights* here – in those tales, there's a woman named Scheherazade who has to keep coming up with stories to tell the King so he doesn't behead her in the morning, like he did to his previous 3,000 wives. It's pretty similar to the way Jane has to keep coming up with ways to tease Rochester and draw out his interest from day to day so that he doesn't…what? Lose interest in her? Lose control and ravish or even rape her? Both of these seem possible at different points in the novel, though Rochester will later claim that he could never have harmed Jane.

We're not saying this is a healthy relationship, but Jane and Rochester seem to like it. They're are always playing with the power dynamic between them: Jane likes to call Rochester her "master" and to "serve" him, but it's also clear that she's stronger – emotionally and ethically – than he is, and that he (this Beast + Bluebeard + Persian King dude) desperately needs her.

Morals? Ethics? I have some of those around here somewhere. Check under the sofa cushions.

Rochester likes to make excuses for himself: he's not a bad person by nature, he was just in a really bad situation with this whole Bertha thing, what could he do but lock her in the attic and sleep his way across Europe, huh? And what's he supposed to do now that he can't get a divorce – just take care of his wife for the rest of her life, considering that he's got all her money anyway and that he shipped her across the Atlantic away from any friends or family who might have helped her? As if! Bigamy is clearly the only reasonable option, right?

Jane's different from all the previous women in Rochester's life because she won't let him get away with that kind of bogus logic. Rochester's long, sophisticated (read: BS) explanations of why his particular situation requires a new and different sort of morality don't convince Jane at all:

[Mr. Rochester:] "[S]ince happiness is irrevocably denied me, I have a right to get pleasure out of life: and I will get it, cost what it may."

[Jane:] "Then you will degenerate still more, sir."

"Possibly: yet why should I, if I can get sweet, fresh pleasure? And I may get it as sweet and fresh as the wild honey the bee gathers on the moor."

"It will sting – it will taste bitter, sir."

"How do you know? – you never tried it. [...] I scarcely think the notion that flittered across my brain was an error. I believe it was an inspiration rather than a temptation: it was very genial, very soothing – I know that. Here it comes again! It is no devil, I assure you; or if it be, it has put on the robes of an angel of light. I think I must admit so fair a guest when it asks entrance to my heart." (1.14.65-71)

Rochester makes two assumptions about ethics here that are different from Jane's: first, that something must be right and good just because it's pleasant, and, second, that moral principles are not absolute and unchanging, but relative to one's situation. Jane doesn't know what he's thinking at this point, but we do: that it couldn't be wrong for him to get romantically involved with her, because he doesn't really have any existing romance in his life and dating Jane would be great. Jane may not be convinced, but perhaps the reader is, just a little bit. We're always willing to overlook some of Rochester's more glaring flaws in order to indulge the passion he and Jane share. That's one of the strange things about *Jane Eyre* being a novel with a didactic side: although Jane always draws a line in the sand and upholds her principles, even the ethically strict Victorian reader might start to see why Rochester's claims for moral relativity make some sense. After all, he did really get shafted by his father and brother when he was young and they tricked him into marrying Bertha.

Blinded By Love (and by a housefire)

It's not surprising that Rochester is injured in the fire that destroys Thornfield Hall, but perhaps it is a little strange that one of his injuries is blindness. With one eye gouged out and the other inflamed, Rochester is uglier than ever, and now he can't see. We'd like to be able to say that he "sees the error of his ways," which is sort of true. At least, Rochester claims that he gets it:

I did wrong: I would have sullied my innocent flower – breathed guilt on its purity: the Omnipotent snatched it from me. [...] Divine justice pursued its course; disasters came thick on me: I was forced to pass through the valley of the shadow of death. His chastisements are mighty; and one smote me which has humbled me for ever. You know I was proud of my strength: but what is it now, when I must give it over to foreign guidance, as a child does its weakness? Of late, Jane – only – only of late – I began to see and acknowledge the hand of God in my doom. I began to experience remorse, repentance; the wish for reconcilement to my Maker. I began sometimes to pray: very brief prayers they were, but very sincere. (3.11.248)

What Rochester seems to understand is that his attempt at bigamy would have negatively impacted Jane ("sullied my innocent flower"). He doesn't think that it negatively impacts him in a moral sense, but at least it's a start.

In literature, there's more to blindness than meets the eye. (Sorry for that one; we couldn't resist.) You may know the legend of Odin, the king of the Norse gods, who traded one of his eyes in exchange for wisdom. Or maybe you know about Tiresias, a Greek prophet who supposedly became blind but gained "inner sight." What we're trying to say is that there's a long mythological and literary tradition of exchanging physical sight for metaphorical sight, and Rochester's blindness alludes to that tradition. It's not a perfect parallel, though; Rochester seems more depressed than enlightened.

So what does it mean that Rochester gets his sense of sight *back* two years after he marries Jane? Perhaps whatever wisdom he gained while dealing with their bad breakup disappears, too, and he goes back to feeling entitled to pleasure and happiness. Perhaps it just means that we need to have miracles at the end of a romance in order to really feel like we're getting that classic happy ending.

Mr. Rochester Timeline and Summary

- Rochester meets Jane and quickly falls in love with her.
- Someone tries to murder Rochester by setting fire to his bed and Jane saves him.
- Rochester invites a bunch of local aristocrats over to his house for a weeks-long party.
- Rochester pretends that he wants to marry Blanche Ingram in order to make Jane jealous.
- When Jane goes to visit her Aunt Reed, Rochester is reluctant to let her leave, but she gives him no choice.
- When Jane comes back to Thornfield, Rochester continues to let her think he's interested in Blanche, and tells Jane she'll have to get another job – in Ireland.
- Eventually, Rochester relents, and asks Jane to marry him. She accepts.
- Rochester tries to give Jane lots of expensive presents while they're engaged, but she refuses.
- Rochester tries to marry Jane, but the wedding is interrupted by two men who reveal his previous marriage to Bertha.
- Rochester shows Bertha to Jane and the men and explains why he was trying to commit bigamy.
- Rochester tries to convince Jane to live with him in France as though they were married. We find out a lot of things about Rochester's past:
- Edward Rochester's father refused to split his estate and left it all to Edward's older brother Rowland.
- Old Mr. Rochester and Rowland developed a plan to make Edward rich: they arranged for him to meet and marry Bertha Mason in the West Indies.
- After he married Bertha, Edward Rochester discovered that insanity ran in her family and that she herself was an insane drunk who liked to sleep around. (At least, that's what he

says about her.)

- Rochester lived with Bertha in the West Indies for four years, but his marriage and life were miserable.
- Rochester's father and brother died and he inherited the family estate.
- Rochester took Bertha back to England and confined her at Thornfield Hall.
- Rochester bummed around Europe taking different mistresses and living it up.
- When one of Rochester's mistresses, Céline Varens, abandoned her daughter Adèle, Rochester adopted the little girl even though she might not be his child.
- Rochester got sick of being a party animal and goes home to England.
- Jane refuses to live with Rochester bigamously and leaves him.
- Ten months later, Jane comes back to Thornfield, and we find out what's been happening to Rochester in the meantime:
- Rochester looked for Jane obsessively for two months, but couldn't find her.
- Rochester became wild and savage and sent Mrs. Fairfax and Adèle away from Thornfield.
- Rochester sulked at Thornfield, practically a hermit.
- When Bertha set fire to the house, Rochester rescued the few servants still living there and tried to rescue Bertha, too, but she committed suicide.
- Rochester was injured in the aftermath of the fire; he lost one hand and one eye, and he's blind in the remaining eye.
- Jane returns to Rochester and they get married.
- After two years, Rochester gets his sight back a little bit.
- Jane and Rochester have a son.

Bertha Mason Character Analysis

Bertha Mason: is she an abused wife, or just "the madwoman in the attic"? Bertha's family heritage is complex and puts her in a difficult position. She's half-Creole and half-English, raised in Jamaica among the British aristocrat half of her family, and already not exactly a part of one world or the other. She also suffers from congenital insanity (read: madness runs in her family). Rochester claims that she was drunken and promiscuous and that her excesses brought on her madness when she was young, but he's not exactly an objective witness.

It's clear that she and Rochester never really got along and that they hadn't gotten to know each other at all before they got married. In that sense, they were both screwed over by their families; they were young and silly, and neither of them really thought to slow down and think about things before saying their vows. As a result of all this, Bertha spends most of her adult life locked in a room – a few years in a room in Jamaica, and ten years in the attic at Thornfield. We don't know about you, but we'd hate the person who did that to us, too.

Bertha's homicidal pyromaniac reaction, however, is admittedly a wee bit extreme. The fact that she crawls around on all fours making animalistic noises and laughing in a creepy way also suggests that the thread of her sanity has long since snapped. However, she's still perceptive in some ways: she figures out that Rochester and Jane are going to get married, and she shows herself to Jane destroying the wedding veil, trying, perhaps to warn her off gently, or at least signal to her that a marriage to Rochester isn't going to work.

"The Madwoman in the Attic"

Bertha has become especially famous in literary criticism because her situation supplied the title and central theory of a major 1979 book of feminist criticism, Sandra Gilbert and Susan Gubar's *The Madwoman in the Attic: The Woman Writer and the Nineteenth-Century Literary Imagination*. Basically, the idea is that the intensely powerful, passionate, and talented woman who is seen as crazy and in need of confinement by the world represents the nineteenth-century woman writer, whose abilities threatened the dominant good-old-boy literary network. Obviously, this has a lot of interesting implications for Bertha as a character, for Charlotte Brontë as an author, and for the "Autobiography" of Jane Eyre.

In Bertha's case, you don't have to know a lot about the Victorian publishing world to get the sense that keeping a woman capable of burning your house down locked upstairs, looming over your whole life is, oh, a little bit symbolic maybe? Something of a skeleton in the closet? Except this skeleton can set fire to things. In fact, Bertha is such an intensely powerful character that even as a prisoner in a remote country house across the ocean from her home, with no friends or family or resources, everyone around her trembles in their boots when she gets loose!

For Charlotte Brontë, Bertha seems to become a strange kind of alter ego. Bertha is rejected by the man who was supposed to love her; Charlotte never married and fell in love with an unattainable man. Bertha is kept prisoner in a lonely house on the English moors; Charlotte traveled a little, but spent most of her life shut up in her father's house in Yorkshire, away from any big-city culture. Bertha is only able to show her powers to the world in what seem like insane, destructive ways; women novelists were common but their works were often considered ridiculous and their abilities inferior to those of men. The parallels are too strong to ignore, and perhaps Bertha does double-duty, both representing the restrictions that Charlotte felt and becoming Charlotte's wish-fulfillment of breaking through those restrictions to inspire fear and awe.

Of course, there's another woman writer here besides Charlotte Brontë – there's Jane Eyre herself, who narrates this entire novel and describes it as her "autobiography." Could Bertha represent Jane if she's also Jane's antagonist? Of course! We're never more like someone than when we consider them our mortal enemy. Think about it: Bertha is locked in a room for ten years and goes crazy "like some wild animal"; Jane is locked in the red-room for five minutes and completely freaks out so that she's "like a mad cat." Bertha sneaks around Thornfield at night to thwart Rochester's plans of remarrying; Jane sneaks around Thornfield at night to thwart Rochester's plans of using her to commit bigamy. Bertha's supposed to be insane; Jane hears voices. So here's the thing: if Jane and Bertha are actually very similar, and if Bertha's pyromaniac madness represents the incendiary potential of the woman writer telling her story, then it seems entirely possible that Jane could end up like Bertha, or that Jane just has the good fortune to be a little more desirable to Rochester and thus escape Bertha's fate.

It's all about perspective

As you probably noticed, everything we learn about Bertha in *Jane Eyre* we learn through Rochester as he's telling the story about her to other people around him. The only things we really "know for a fact" because we as readers have seen them are that Bertha is violent toward

Rochester and her brother, that she's extremely disturbed in some way if not actually insane, and that she's kept locked in the attic. Given Rochester's moral sensibilities, it seems only fair to suggest that we can't really judge Bertha without knowing her side of the story, which we don't get in *Jane Eyre*. To address this gap, in 1966 Jean Rhys explored what Bertha's perspective might be like in a novel called *Wide Sargasso Sea*. While it doesn't necessarily make sense to use that novel in a paper that's just about what's going on in the text of *Jane Eyre*, it is a fascinating re-imagining of the situation that makes us think more deeply about the issues of race and inequality at stake here. We highly recommend it!

Bertha Mason Timeline and Summary

- Rochester tells us Bertha's back-story (printed here in italics):
- *Bertha is a young debutante in Jamaica, where all the boys love her and her beauty and musical talent make her extremely desirable.*
- Bertha's family and Edward Rochester's family arrange for their marriage.
- Bertha is mentally unstable and (apparently) unhappy, and she behaves erratically, screaming at servants, drinking a lot, and sleeping around.
- Bertha is diagnosed as insane and kept in a locked room.
- After four years of marriage, Rochester takes Bertha back to England and confines her at Thornfield with Grace Poole as her nurse and jailer.
- Bertha remains at Thornfield tended only by Grace for ten years.
- Rochester comes back to Thornfield, bringing his ward Adèle and a governess, Jane Eyre.
- Bertha becomes aware of Rochester's attachment to Jane.
- Bertha sneaks past a drunk Grace Poole and sets fire to Rochester's bed in the middle of the night.
- Bertha's brother shows up to visit her; he tries to talk to her alone, but she stabs and bites him.
- Bertha sneaks out of her room again and goes to Jane's bedroom. Bertha examines Jane's wedding dress and honeymoon luggage and tears her veil in half.
- Rochester shows Bertha to Jane, a lawyer, and Bertha's brother and describes her condition. Bertha behaves like a wild animal and tries to bite Rochester's face.
- Bertha sets fire to Jane's old bed in the middle of the night and burns Thornfield down. As it's burning, she climbs up onto a high wall and jumps off before Rochester can stop her, effectively committing suicide.

St. John Rivers Character Analysis

The first thing to explain about St. John Rivers is how to pronounce his first name, "St. John." It's not "Saint John," although of course that's what it means; it's pronounced "SIN-jun." Don't ask us why this is; the British have this thing about silly pronunciation. He's not actually a saint, either – it's just a weird first name – although he does think that he's one of the elect. (Also, while we're talking about names, it might be worth thinking about Jane's two different cousins named John – John Reed and St. John Rivers – together for a moment.)

St. John may not have been officially canonized as a saint yet, but he's pretty convinced that he's close to it. After all, he's done some serious mortifying of the flesh in order to sacrifice all his desires and become a missionary in India. Mostly, this makes sense; he just isn't happy living calm, normal domestic life. He has that drive that some people get to go out and prove themselves against strange challenges and unbearable odds. But there is one thing he hasn't been able to stop himself from wanting: Miss Rosamond Oliver, the local wealthy beauty. She loves him, he loves her, her dad is OK with it – it should work out. And St. John basically turns into Jell-O every time he sees her. He thinks, though, that she'd be a bad missionary wife, and so he refuses to let himself act on his feelings for her. Giving up the missionary-in-India project just isn't possible.

Apart from this one passion, St. John is "hard and cold," he's "frozen over," he's "cold as an iceberg." He may be handsome, blonde, and blue-eyed, but he might as well be "no longer flesh, but marble" – like some kind of Greek statue of Apollo. When he proposes to Jane, who he thinks would make a great missionary wife, she's appalled by the idea that he would marry someone he doesn't love. She also knows that he'd even force himself to have sex with her, because that's what husbands and wives do, despite not having any warm feelings for her. Jane finds the whole thing disgusting, and so do we.

The strange thing about St. John is that he might at first seem like an obsessive-compulsive, cold-blooded freak, but actually he is what Jane's been trying to become: someone who makes relationship decisions based only on logic and practicality. Once Jane realizes that he's the natural end point of that philosophy, she goes running back to her true love, Rochester, as fast as she can, Bertha or no Bertha.

Remember, *Jane Eyre* ends with St. John Rivers; he's the last character we think about, alone out there in India, missionary-ing and stuff. There tends to be a lot of emphasis on endings in literature, so that's probably important. (See "What's Up With the Ending?")

St. John Rivers Timeline and Summary

- St. John is living at Moor House with his sisters Diana and Mary; he works as the clergyman in the nearby town of Morton while preparing to go to India on a missionary trip.
- St. John comes home one night to find a poor young woman begging on the doorstep of Moor House; he invites her in and lets his sisters give her something to eat and a bed for the night.
- St. John gets to know this young woman – Jane Eyre. He arranges for her to teach a village girls' school in Morton and to have a cottage.
- St. John stifles his passion for local beauty Rosamond Oliver and asks Jane to marry him instead because she would be a better missionary's wife. Jane refuses.
- St. John pressures Jane to marry him for several weeks, but Jane continues refusing. Just as she's about to give in, something changes her attitude and she resists.

- St. John leaves Moor House and goes to Cambridge for two weeks to say goodbye to friends before leaving for India.
- St. John returns to Moor House only to find that Jane is gone. He receives a letter from her saying that she has married Mr. Rochester.
- St. John goes to India and undertakes his missionary work. After a long period of labor, he becomes sick in the extreme climate of India and expects to die soon.

Mrs. Reed Character Analysis

Jane's aunt-by-marriage is a selfish, hard-hearted woman who spoils her three horrible children, John, Eliza, and Georgiana, and hates her niece. Mrs. Reed's dislike of Jane is only increased when Jane actually stands up for herself and rejects her aunt's cruelty and oppression. In terms of the plot of the novel, Mrs. Reed performs two major functions. First, she is Jane's childhood antagonist, and the experience of dealing with her cultivates Jane's hatred of injustice. Later in the novel, when she's dying, Mrs. Reed becomes an opportunity for Jane to show that she has learned a lesson about Christian forgiveness from her friendship with Helen Burns.

Helen Burns Character Analysis

Helen is Jane's pious best friend at Lowood Institute. Helen is extremely intelligent, calm, and caring, but her most important aspect is her devout religious faith. If *Jane Eyre* were an allegory, Helen would basically be a walking version of the New Testament instructions to "turn the other cheek" and "bless them that curse you" and "love your enemies." Constantly victimized by the nasty teacher Miss Scatcherd, Helen never seems to take offense at the way she's treated and even tries to see things from Miss Scatcherd's perspective. Jane is confused by Helen's patient, loving response to mistreatment, but she's also awed by Helen's brilliance and knowledge. Of course, a character this virtuous really couldn't make it very far into the novel without dying in a tragic yet beautiful way. Maybe it seems less like a formulaic plot device when you know that Helen was based on Charlotte Brontë's sister Maria, who died young.

Mr. Brocklehurst Character Analysis

The ultimate hypocrite, Mr. Brocklehurst is the supervisor of a boarding school for orphaned girls, Lowood Institute, which was founded by one of his relatives. Mr. Brocklehurst gets his kicks in life from going around intimidating little girls, keeping them half-starved and cold, and telling them that they're going to hell for their sins, all while feeling self-righteous about doing it and thinking that God's giving him a big thumbs-up. Of course, Mr. Brocklehurst's own children wear silk and fur and we're sure they've never missed a meal in their life, but apparently (in *their* opinion), God's chill with that.

Miss Temple Character Analysis

Miss Temple, the teacher in charge of Lowood Institute, is the only person able to protect the girls at the school from the cruelty of Mr. Brocklehurst. Miss Temple gains Jane's loyalty forever when she takes steps to find out whether Jane really is a liar, as Mr. Brocklehurst and Mrs. Reed claim, or not. There's really not much to Miss Temple's character, but she's important to Jane's development as someone who takes the trouble to care about the truth and who encourages Jane to apply herself to her education. She also has a semi-allegorical aspect; for eight years, she basically is Jane's place of refuge (get it – *Temple*?), and, when she leaves Lowood, Jane is ready to leave, too.

John Reed Character Analysis

Jane's cousin John Reed is a good-for-nothing wastrel. As a child, he's a bully, pushing Jane around, reminding her of her poverty, and trying to keep her from enjoying herself in any way despite the fact that he's four years older than her and should really be a little more mature. What kind of fourteen-year-old boy needs to push around his ten-year-old female cousin in order to feel good about himself? As an adult, John Reed is a complete waste of space; all he does is spend money, gamble, get into debt, fail out of college, go to brothels, sponge off his mom, threaten to commit suicide, and threaten to hurt his own mom if she doesn't keep giving him money. When he finally does commit suicide, only Mrs. Reed misses him. He doesn't really have any redeeming features whatsoever, which makes him a pretty flat character, but it's important that Jane learns to stand up to him.

Eliza Reed Character Analysis

In childhood, Jane's cousin Eliza is just another nasty member of the Reed family; as an adult, she becomes more and more prim, proper, and repressed as she jealously watches all the boys flock to her sister Georgiana. Eventually, she's turned herself into a robot, with every fifteen-minute period of every day of her life scheduled and organized, and no friendships or romances or loving relationships of any kind. When her mother dies, she moves to France and becomes a nun. The novel wants us to think about her as pretty wrongheaded in this decision; instead of dealing with her jealousy and disappointment, she tries to cut emotion entirely out of her life and spend her whole life being blank and detached. Hmm, does that sound like any other characters we meet later in the novel? Yep, Eliza Reed prepares us (and Jane!) for St. John Rivers. One major difference: one of Eliza's problems is that she doesn't become a nun because she feels called to serve God, but because she wants to get away from the world. St. John at least has a genuine "calling" to be a missionary.

Georgiana Reed Character Analysis

Georgiana Reed, sister of Eliza and John, daughter of Mrs. Reed, and cousin to Jane Eyre, is completely different from her sister. A plump, lovely blonde, Georgiana has plenty of admirers and romances, and would have eloped with a lord if her sister hadn't ratted her out. She's completely selfish, talks only about herself and superficial little details of her life, and doesn't seem to really understand or even care about her brother's death and her mother's illness. Eliza has dismissed happiness and pleasure; Georgiana has dismissed everything else. Together, the two of them represent extreme reactions to the difficult problem of balancing passion and rationality.

Bessie Character Analysis

Bessie is Jane's childhood nursemaid; she's not exactly perfect, because she has a hot temper and behaves pretty inconsistently to Jane (sometimes bringing her treats, sometimes punishing her for nothing at all with a smack, sometimes forgetting her completely for a bit), but she's the closest thing Jane has to a mother or an ally when she's living at Gateshead. For a minor character, Bessie is actually considerably developed; we see her compassion, her impatience, her temper, and her affection for Jane all at once. One result of this well-rounded characterization of a servant early in the novel is to prepare us for the idea that class status doesn't necessarily have a direct relationship to importance or complexity in *Jane Eyre*; the lady of the house might be a flat, boring character, and her maid could be the really interesting one.

Blanche Ingram Character Analysis

Blanche Ingram is, let's be honest, not a nice girl. The daughter of one of Rochester's distant neighbors, Blanche gets interested in him because of his fortune and because she thinks an ugly husband would be easy to dominate. She's a beautiful, selfish snob with a serious attitude problem. Her name, "Blanche," clues us in a little bit – she's related to the color white, as in pure and cold, but also a blank, someone with no real personality. Still, Rochester uses Blanche somewhat unfairly; he makes it look to everyone as though he's going to marry her just to make Jane jealous. He thinks leading Blanche on is OK because she was a gold-digger anyway, but Jane is frustrated with his behavior.

Adèle Character Analysis

Adèle is Jane's pupil at Thornfield, a little French girl just under ten years old, the daughter of Céline Varens, an opera dancer who was Rochester's mistress. Mostly, Adèle is an opportunity for Jane to show her teaching skills and her compassion. When Jane first meets her, she's only been in England for a few months, and she's never really been asked to study or apply herself; all she really cares about are clothes and getting attention by showing off her singing and dancing skills (all learned from her mom, so mostly inappropriately mature for a little girl). This gives her a little bit of a creepy Lolita feel, but it never fully manifests.

It's not clear whether Adèle is actually Rochester's daughter. Things that suggest she is: her mom said she was, Rochester was sleeping with Céline at the time Adèle was conceived, and he felt ethically obligated to take care of Adèle when her mom abandoned her. Things that suggest she isn't: both Rochester and Jane think that Adèle doesn't look or act like him at all, and Céline was cheating on Rochester at the time Adèle was conceived. Too bad there wasn't any DNA testing available in the nineteenth century; we need Maury Povitch to sort this one out.

Adèle does grow and develop as a character; at the very end of the novel, Jane tells us about the various stages of Adèle's education, which start to resemble Jane's education quite a bit:

You have not quite forgotten little Adèle, have you, reader? I had not; I soon asked and obtained leave of Mr. Rochester, to go and see her at the school where he had placed her. Her frantic joy at beholding me again moved me much. She looked pale and thin: she said she was not happy. I found the rules of the establishment were too strict, its course of study too severe for a child of her age: I took her home with me. I meant to become her governess once more, but I soon found this impracticable; my time and cares were now required by another – my husband needed them all. So I sought out a school conducted on a more indulgent system, and near enough to permit of my visiting her often, and bringing her home sometimes. I took care she should never want for anything that could contribute to her comfort: she soon settled in her new abode, became very happy there, and made fair progress in her studies. As she grew up, a sound English education corrected in a great measure her French defects; and when she left school, I found in her a pleasing and obliging companion: docile, good-tempered, and well-principled. (3.12.11)

Maybe the cycle is starting all over again: just as Jane suffered under the strict discipline and neglect at Lowood, Adèle has a similar unpleasant boarding school experience that seems to turn her into a useful, principled English girl.

Grace Poole Character Analysis

Grace Poole, a stout, middle-aged, red-haired seamstress who works as a servant at Thornfield Hall, is secretly the nursemaid and prison guard for the insane Bertha Mason. Jane keeps assuming that Grace is responsible for the eerie laugh on the third floor, the attempt to burn Rochester alive, and other strange and creepy nighttime deeds. Grace's main function in the novel is as a red herring, a piece of misdirection. If this were *The Wizard of Oz,* Grace would be the giant head of the wizard, and Bertha would be the man behind the curtain.

Diana and Mary Rivers Character Analysis

St. John's sisters and Jane's cousins, Diana and Mary Rivers are gentle, compassionate, educated young women who take to Jane immediately. Mary doesn't have much personality, but Diana is a natural leader and teacher. Diana teaches German to both Jane and Mary and her firm insistence on Jane's place in their household begins to push Jane and St. John together.

Rosamond Oliver Character Analysis

Rosamond Oliver is the beautiful young woman that St. John is not-so-secretly in love with, but won't allow himself to marry because she wouldn't make a good missionary wife. We suspect that he also enjoys torturing himself by denying his passion for her. For some time, Rosamond seems to hope that St. John will ask her to marry him, but eventually she takes a practical approach, gives up, and marries someone else. We can't really blame her.

Character Roles

Protagonist
Jane Eyre
What's to say? This is Jane's story. She's telling it, it's named after her, and we follow her every step of the way.

Antagonist
Mrs. Reed
Jane's Aunt Reed is sort of like a trial antagonist before the main action of the plot really gets going. She's like the character version of tapping a microphone and saying "testing, testing, one, two, three." What's important for Jane is to be able to recognize that Mrs. Reed is her antagonist, not just a powerful adult who's right all the time. It's no accident that the novel begins as soon as she figures that out: only when Jane realizes that Mrs. Reed is the bad guy (er, gal) can Jane herself become the heroine of her own story.

Antagonist
Bertha Mason
It's interesting to think about Bertha as Jane's antagonist – after all, Jane only sees Bertha twice, and neither time do they really talk to each other or anything (not that Bertha's a big conversationalist anyway). But Bertha comes to represent everything that's keeping Jane away from the man she loves, and Bertha's weird nighttime activities are a passive-aggressive way of driving Jane away from Thornfield. Or maybe they're an aggressive-aggressive way of doing it: tearing a wedding veil in half is pretty obvious.

Think of it this way: it's the old versus the new. Nicole Kidman vs. Katie Holmes. Katie Couric vs. Kelly Ripa. It's a catfight between the plain, dignified young Englishwoman and the crazed harlot from overseas! Ack! Yeah, we thought that would bother you. It bothers us, too. We think Bertha might be getting the short end of the stick on this deal, and there might be just a wee bit of prejudice against first wives, older women, and anyone who's not English.

Antagonist
Mr. Rochester
Wait a minute, you're saying: Mr. Rochester is Jane's *love interest,* not her enemy. But her enemy is exactly what he becomes when he tries to wheedle her into becoming his mistress. However he excuses or explains it, Jane knows that he's trying to tempt her – and himself –

into ignoring some basic moral principles, and she won't let him get away with it. She's made weaker in her struggle against him by her youth, inexperience, solitude, poverty, and financial dependence on him – but luckily she has more than enough sass to make up for all those deficiencies.

Antagonist

St. John Rivers

St. John is Jane's final challenge. Finding out that Jane still has to fight St. John even after making the big decision to leave Mr. Rochester is sort of like finding out that Beowulf still has to face Grendel's mother even after killing Grendel. (Don't know what we're talking about? Go and read Shmoop's coverage of *Beowulf*!) St. John isn't just Jane's antagonist because he wants her to marry him and she's not interested; he's also an extreme version of what Jane has been trying to become – a dispassionate, rational person guided only by calm consideration of morality and ethics. Jane has to reject him and embrace her own passionate nature before she can marry Rochester.

Guide/Mentor

Helen Burns

Helen is Jane's first real guide and mentor. As Jane's peer, she first gets Jane's interest because she's studious and virtuous and doesn't seem bothered by the injustices of Lowood. Helen is able to let injustice roll of her like water of a duck's back, and Jane can't understand why. Although Jane never really agrees completely with Helen's "turn the other cheek" philosophy, Helen's example shows her the wonders of education and the power of strong morality and religious faith.

Guide/Mentor

Jane Eyre

We know it seems a little odd to consider Jane as her own guide and mentor, but in this novel that's exactly what happens. Although Jane does find a few friends and mentors as a student at Lowood (Helen Burns and Miss Temple) and some friends at Moor House (Diana and Mary Rivers), for most of the novel, she relies entirely on herself for moral, spiritual, and practical guidance. Jane has to think up a plan to get a job all on her own; she has to figure out how to do that job on her own; she has to figure out how to conduct her romance with Rochester all on her own; and she has to decide whether to make a moral stand against his attempt at bigamy completely alone. Jane is her own moral touchstone most of the time, and that's that.

Foil

Bertha Mason to Jane Eyre

Bertha and Jane only meet face-to-face twice, and they never have any conversations, but, as Rochester's two wives and as the two higher-class-than-the-servants residents of Thornfield, they're still odd doubles of one another. Both are in many ways outsiders or "Others," both have passionate sexual desires for Rochester, and both seem a little bit eerie or supernatural. Of course, Jane's a sometimes-mild-mannered plain-faced English girl of eighteen, and Bertha's a crazy Creole woman twice Jane's age, but what's really weird is that these major differences start to pale in comparison to their similarities. And that makes us ask: could Jane ever share Bertha's fate? She seems to think it's possible when she tells Rochester that she knows he'll get tired of her after a year.

Foil
St. John Rivers to Mr. Rochester
Though St. John and Rochester never meet, we're definitely contrasting their different relationships to Jane in our heads all through Book III of the novel. Jane rejects Rochester's illicit passion and his attempt to commit bigamy and/or make her his mistress, but she's even more appalled by St. John's desire to make her his legal wife and sexual partner without love or passion. St. John may be more correct in the eyes of the law and the Lord, but the demands he makes of Jane are much more disgusting than Rochester's. Remember, Jane goes back to Rochester not because she knows he's single now but because she's got to get away from St. John.

Romantic Interest
Mr. Rochester
What's interesting about this isn't really that Rochester is Jane's love interest – that's true, but so what? The interesting thing is that it takes us a long time as readers to readjust to the idea that Rochester could be Jane's honey instead of her money.

Character Clues

Direct Characterization
Jane's often pretty straightforward in telling us her impressions and opinions of people, everything from what they look like to how they behave, starting with John Reed, whom she describes explicitly as a bully. Even when she's a child she gives us the scoop on everybody around her: "John had not much affection for his mother and sisters, and an antipathy to me." "Eliza...was headstrong and selfish." "Georgiana...had a spoiled temper, a very acrid sprite, a captious and insolent carriage." These descriptions are, of course, a little tricky; we have to take them with a grain of salt, since they come through a character and not directly from an impersonal, third-person narrator.

Thoughts and Opinions
Most of the characters in *Jane Eyre* are opinionated, and nearly all of them share their attitudes with Jane by telling them to her (or stating them in front of her) directly. Blanche Ingram's opinion that the best husbands are subservient shows her own self-importance and need to dominate others. Mrs. Reed's opinion that Jane was a troublesome, unnatural child shows her own unhappiness and tendency to find fault with anyone who isn't her relative or her inferior. St. John's opinion that he can't marry Rosamond Oliver because she wouldn't be a good missionary wife shows us his obsession with asceticism and self-denial.

Social Status
Jane's position as a governess clues us in to the fact that she approaches almost every relationship as though she were a student trying to learn something or a teacher trying to get someone else to learn something. The in-between-ness of being a governess – sort of like a member of the family because you're better educated than the servants, but sort of like a servant because you're a paid employee – reminds us once again of Jane's ability to move

between worlds and social spheres and the difficulty of really labeling or placing her once and for all.

Names
Jane *Eyre* – it sounds like "air," or "heir," or "ear." So we know that Jane has "airy-fairy" aspects, that her "air" (her deportment or manners) is particularly important, that she might sometimes "give herself airs" or be a little snobby, that there's probably a moment in which she inherits something and becomes an "heir," that she's a good listener – an "ear" for everyone around her, and maybe able to hear unusual things. Her first name, Jane, sounds plain and unremarkable at first – and she seems plain and unremarkable *at first* too. But it's not just Jane who is characterized by her name – Rochester's name is related to an obsolete word meaning "rock," *roche,* which reminds us of his craggy, hard-featured face, his lack of manners, and his harsh demands. And St. John Rivers...obviously there's the whole St. John thing, plus a sense of the "river of God." We're sure you can do " *Blanche* Ingram" on your own.

Physical Appearances
Jane's plain looks tell us that she's an unaffected, unpretentious, genuine person. And about Rochester's ugliness, is there a *wee* bit of a chance that he might be the "Beast" half of a "Beauty and the Beast" sort of story? (Only this one is "Plain Jane and the Beast"...doesn't really have the same ring to it, does it?) St. John's strange paleness alerts us to his cold-blooded, stern, passionless attitude. You get the idea. We're more interested in the moments where appearances don't seem as significant: Blanche Ingram's beauty doesn't mean she's a good person, for example.

Clothing
Clothing is a constant tool of characterization in *Jane Eyre*, from the plain dresses the girls wear at Lowood all the way to Jane's insistence on a wedding veil that's not too fancy. For example, when Jane insists on continuing to wear her plain gray and black gowns instead of starting to dress in gaudy, expensive, brightly-colored dresses Rochester wants to purchase, it shows us that she's refusing to turn into his mistress.

Literary Devices

Symbols, Imagery, Allegory

The Red-Room
The red-room, once the bedroom of Jane's Uncle Reed, was (we're sure you remember) the chamber in which he died. Locked in the red-room, believing that her uncle's ghost is manifesting, Jane experiences a moment of extreme trauma leading to hysteria. So let's think about this: Jane's *Aunt*, an older woman who is supposed to be like a foster mother to her but is more like an evil stepmother, locks Jane into a room that's entirely decorated in red with a little bit of white, and Jane panics when she thinks that an older male relative's ghost might be invading the room. Hmm, we're not going to have to go too far to do some psychoanalyzing here, are we? For example, on the most extreme end, you could claim that the red-room is like

a womb, and Aunt Reed is infantilizing Jane and forcing her back into the womb to be born again with, needless to say, a new attitude. (If this is the case, of course it's alarming when a male relative invades the womb, right?) We know, we know, that sounds a little silly, but when you think about it, it actually makes a little sense. Some less-wacky interpretations: that the red-room is a space in which the purity and innocence of childhood (the white bits) meet the intense and bitter emotions that come with unpleasant life experience – anger, fear, and anxiety (the red bits). Think of Jane as "seeing red" at this moment. Alternatively, you can think about the red-room experience as part of the indescribable trauma of suffering; remember, Jane loses consciousness because she can hardly deal with it, and she can never quite verbalize what the problem is (besides the possibility of a ghost). Whenever Jane suffers in the future, it will take her, emotionally, back to the red-room.

Gross Porridge

That's a symbol? Yep, sure is. There are two important moments when really nasty porridge figures in Jane's life. The first is at Lowood, when Jane arrives and, along with the other girls, is served burnt porridge for breakfast. It's so disgusting that nobody can eat it, and Miss Temple ends up giving the girls an extra meal during the day to make up for it, which pisses off Mr. Brocklehurst. The second is during Jane's period of homeless wandering, when a woman and a little girl tending a pig give Jane a bowl of cold, hard, congealed porridge that the pig wouldn't eat. So what does it symbolize? Well, basically, a level of humility and subjection that's unnatural for anyone to attain. Mr. Brocklehurst thinks that, if the girls are served inedible porridge, they should either (a) eat it and be grateful anyway and "mortify the flesh" or (b) go hungry and use the opportunity to "mortify the flesh." We can tell, however, that he's never missed a meal in his life and that either of those options is a cruel martyrdom, not a real opportunity for spiritual growth. When Jane is forced to take the congealed porridge and be grateful for it later in the novel, we realize she's been brought down to the very low level that someone like Mr. Brocklehurst (or Mrs. Reed!) wanted her to occupy. We're meant, of course, to be quite alarmed about this.

Fire

The most important fires in *Jane Eyre* are Bertha's two acts of arson: the first at the end of Book I (Chapter 15), when Bertha sets fire to Rochester's bedclothes, and the second at the end of Book III (Chapter 10), when Jane learns that Bertha managed to burn down Thornfield by setting fire to what was once Jane's bedroom. She's a real pyromaniac, that Bertha. Anyway, let's repeat that first one in case you missed it: *Bertha sets fire to Rochester's bedclothes.* Since we know that one of the main problems in Bertha and Rochester's marriage was that, even though she was beautiful and attractive – Rochester tells us that she was "in the style of Blanche Ingram" – she had a rapacious sexual appetite. She was "unchaste" and "dragged" Rochester through "hideous and degrading agonies." To translate that out of the polite nineteenth-century jargon, she cheated on him a bunch and everybody knew about it. The sexual desire Rochester originally felt for Bertha, the sexual attention she drew from a crowd of admiring men, and her affairs – all of this sets his *bed on fire*, nudge, nudge. Jane extinguishes the literal flames only to kindle new ones of a metaphorical kind!

When, much later, Bertha takes her pyro tendencies to Jane's bedroom, she seems to be objecting directly to Jane's own sexual interest in Rochester – but also, perhaps, *transferring* her highly-sexed nature to Jane. Don't forget that Jane calls herself "fire" when she's talking to

St. John Rivers – one more thing she and Bertha actually have in common. Bertha's arson also symbolizes her using the power of sexuality to destroy Rochester's home; Thornfield actually burning down is a real-world parallel to its metaphorical burning – Jane's abandonment of Rochester after his desire for her caused him to attempt bigamy.

Ice

If you've read *Frankenstein*, then you know that, where there's fire, there's also ice! (OK, you could learn that from Robert Frost, too.) Anyway, not only does Jane take special interest in the images of birds in arctic landscapes when she's reading *Bewick's British Birds* as a child, as an adult she draws a fantasy landscape filled with ice and snow that seems to have special meaning for her. When she decides that she has to leave Rochester, she tells herself that she "must be ice and rock to him" instead of letting him know that she returns his passion. Of course, the iciest of the characters isn't Jane herself, but St. John Rivers, who has an "ice of reserve" and claims that "no fervour infects" him. (Later, Jane tells Rochester that St. John is "cold as an iceberg.") Jane's fascination with ice seems to be the result of her hotheaded nature – she herself may seem cold, but she's actually incredibly fiery and passionate, and she gets really angry about injustice. As a result, she's mesmerized by all things frozen and icy, because she can't be that way. Her one attempt at icy behavior – rejecting Rochester – results in her meeting St. John, who shows her just how undesirable a cold-hearted approach to the world really is. In fact, St. John's lack of passion seems almost immoral.

The Splintered Chestnut Tree

The day after Rochester proposes to Jane under "the great horse-chestnut at the bottom of the orchard," that same tree gets "struck by lightning in the night, and half of it split away" (2.8.119). It can't be a good omen to have something that's whole get violently split in half right after two people sitting beside it decide to unite themselves. The real question is whether the tree represents Jane and Rochester or just Rochester. If the tree represents the two of them and their union, then the half that gets split away is Jane, who is driven away from Rochester by her own desire to avoid temptation. But much later in the novel, Rochester compares himself to the splintered tree and Jane to a new plant: "I am no better than the old lightning-struck chestnut-tree in Thornfield orchard…And what right would that ruin have to bid a budding woodbine cover its decay with freshness?" (3.11.109) The point is not to make you choose between these two interpretations of the symbol, but to suggest that they coexist: the tree represents Rochester, but also Rochester and Jane together, because Rochester can't be himself without her, and because he'll never recover completely from the trauma of their separation (just like the tree will never be the same after getting struck by lightning).

"The Madwoman in the Attic"

The phrase "the madwoman in the attic" is the invention of two famous feminist literary critics, Sandra Gilbert and Susan Gubar, who wrote a book with that title in 1979. (See "Brain Snacks" for more on the book.) The phrase, of course, refers specifically to Bertha Mason, Rochester's sometime wife, now an insane prisoner locked in the attic of his house with Grace Poole for a nursemaid. Gilbert and Gubar develop a critical theory about this "madwoman in the attic" figure: she represents all the subverted rage and pain experienced by the female author of the text (in this case, Charlotte Brontë). Bertha can be locked away, kept secret, and labeled as insane, but nobody can deny her intensity or power: she's sexually potent, wicked smart, and absolutely ruthless. Nobody can kill her, either, because she seems to be invincible – in this novel, of course, she chooses to commit suicide. If Bertha is representative of Charlotte, then what might it mean for Charlotte to kill off her evil doppelgänger as she's writing?

Drawing Portraits

Jane draws four crucial portraits over the course of the novel: one of herself, one of what she imagines Blanche Ingram will look like, one of Rochester, and one of Rosamond Oliver. The first two she draws at the same time so that she can compare them and remind herself how plain and pathetic she is. The one of Rochester she draws almost unconsciously while back at Gateshead caring for the dying Mrs. Reed. (After all, if you don't have a snapshot of your sweetie on your cell phone, then sketching his portrait is probably the best you can do.) Rosamond Oliver's picture she tries to use to get St. John to admit his feelings for that woman. Jane's ability to capture likenesses of herself and those around her reminds us of her flair for narrative description and for penetrating analyses of the people she knows. In the plot of the novel, Jane may be sketching actual portraits – but in the text of the novel, she sketches those portraits, too, just in a more active sense. Jane's artistic skill reminds us of her storytelling abilities and of the careful crafting that goes into her tale – perhaps a craft that's sometimes rather *crafty* and even a bit misleading.

Setting

Nineteenth-Century Rural England: Gateshead, Lowood Institute, Thornfield/Millcote, the moors, Moor House/Morton, Ferndean

Most of the place names we get in *Jane Eyre* are fictitious: they're the names of houses (Gateshead Hall, where the Reeds live; Thornfield Hall and Ferndean Manor, Mr. Rochester's places; and Moor House, where the Rivers siblings live) or schools (Lowood Institute) or little imaginary towns (Millcote, Morton) that resemble lots of places in nineteenth-century north-central England, but we never really get any specifics on where exactly we are other than that. It's sort of like the British equivalent of setting something in "the Midwest" – it's a general region with a certain feel to it, but not a specific place like Kansas. Jane never even goes to London, which would at least be a real English city. (London is far south of where she is in the novel.) On a more specific level, each of Jane's settings provides a pair of indoor and outdoor spaces for her to range in: Gateshead and the walk outside, Lowood and the woods/marshes, Thornfield and its garden and woods, and the moors that stretch between Thornfield and Morton. So Jane's always able to move fluidly between the natural world and human civilization – just one more of her strange, fairy-like abilities to cross boundaries.

Each of the imaginary-but-specific houses or places where Jane lives represent a certain stage in her life. Her childhood happens at Gateshead and ends (mostly) when she reaches her ethical awakening with the red-room incident. Notice the name, "Gateshead" – this place is her "gateway" or entrance to the rest of the world and the "head" or fount of all her problems. She then moves on to her education at Lowood Institute until she wants to get out into the world and seek her fortune. "Lowood" meaning "low wood," because that's where the place is built (in a low valley beside a wood) but also because it's a "low" time in her life. Next comes young love at Thornfield, where she finds mystery and temptation – a "field of thorns" with an almost allegorical or Biblical flavor. Then Jane endures a temporary banishment at Moor House and in the little town of Morton, where she discovers friends and relatives in unlikely places and recharges herself. It's no accident that she's able to rest up for her final adventure "out on the moors," in the wilderness, which also has a religious flavor. Finally, Jane experiences mature love at Ferndean when she returns to Rochester. Jane can't just go back to her naive young love after the experiences she's had; Thornfield has to be burned down once and for all and a new "ferny brae" or Eden-like paradise appears.

It's also important to notice the effect of some nineteenth-century beliefs and customs on the novel. In a novel from a later time period, the central problem of bigamy wouldn't even exist, because Rochester would be able to get a divorce from Bertha and move on with his life. Britain's relationship with its colonies, especially India and the West Indies, and the effects of imperial rule on British culture are also in evidence, as are nineteenth-century ideas about disease (the "miasma theory," which suggests that disease is caused by unhealthy fogs and mists instead of germs) and about character ("phrenology," a pseudo-science that claimed you could tell someone's character type from the shape of their face and skull, which was widely believed at the time).

Narrator Point of View

First Person (Central Narrator)
The narrative point-of-view seems pretty straightforward here: our protagonist, Jane Eyre, tells us her own story in a novel called *Jane Eyre*. It's written in the first person, and the central character is doing the talking (or maybe writing). But Jane is – well, not exactly an unreliable narrator (in fact, she pays a lot of attention to giving us accurate detail), but sometimes you have to read between the lines. Jane's pretty good at telling us what's going on around her, but not always too good at telling us what's going on in her head. Oh, sure, she explains how she makes decisions, and sometimes even explains how she feels – but sometimes she seems a little too modest, like she's suppressing her most intense feelings to try and seem calmer or more composed. Think about the part of the novel (Book III, Chapter I) where Rochester tells Jane his history up until the point he met her and the way he describes his own impression of Jane when she first came to Thornfield:

"I found you full of strange contrasts. Your garb and manner were restricted by rule; your air was often diffident, and altogether that of one refined by nature, but absolutely unused to society, and a good deal afraid of making herself disadvantageously conspicuous by some solecism or blunder; yet when addressed, you lifted a keen, a daring, and a glowing eye to your interlocutor's face: there was penetration and power in each glance you gave; when plied by close questions, you found ready and round answers. [...] There was something glad in your glance, and genial in your manner, when you conversed: I saw you had a social heart; it was the silent schoolroom – it was the tedium of your life – that made you mournful." (3.1.100)

Rochester claims that Jane may be stern and repressed, but he says he can tell this is just the effect of being at Lowood as a teacher and student for a really long time, and that with the right company Jane will loosen up a little. We think he's right, but we would never have figured that out from Jane's own self-presentation in the rest of the narrative. So, even though we can trust Jane on most things, she's not always her own best psychoanalyst.

Genre

Coming-of-Age, Romance, Gothic Fiction, Mystery, Autobiography

We know, that's five genres – but *Jane Eyre* is a complex book, OK? Think about it – there's the whole following-Jane-from-her-sad-childhood-as-an-orphan-to-her-happy-marriage thing, which definitely sounds like a "Coming-of-Age" story to us, especially because at every stage we're focused on her developing morals and ethics.

Jane's passionate attachment to Rochester definitely makes this qualify as a "Romance" – think of all the times Rochester grasps her and clasps her to his chest. Whew! We get hot and steamy just thinking about it.

Then there are all the supernatural and "Gothic Fiction" elements. Even though most of them get explained away – Bertha may look like a vampire, but she's just a woman from Jamaica struck with madness – the novel depends on making us feel that creepy, suspenseful atmosphere.

There's definitely a strong "Mystery" quality here; like a younger version of Agatha Christie's Miss Marple (whose first name, we'd like to point out, is also Jane), Jane gradually unravels Rochester's seedy past to figure out what's going on in the attic at Thornfield.

Then there's the issue of "Autobiography," which is the subtitle: after all, the novel is called *Jane Eyre: An Autobiography*. Because this is a first-person novel, our protagonist describes herself as though she's telling us her autobiography...but since she's not real, it isn't exactly one. We talk about that more in "What's Up With the Title?" So, yes, there are a lot of genres at work here.

Tone

Transparent, Affectionate, Subtle

Because there is so much autobiographical material in *Jane Eyre*, it's often difficult to separate Charlotte Brontë's authorial tone from the narrative style of her protagonist. Often the author's voice and attitude seem to get caught up in the story, making it more like a memoir than a novel. We're calling this a "transparent" tone, where we seem to be looking straight through the author's personality at the first-person narrator. When something of Brontë's own personality starts to come through, it's usually in dialogue, when another character is talking to Jane. Mr. Rochester and Diana Rivers, for example, seem to be two of the characters who occasionally express the author's attitude toward Jane herself. For example, when Jane says that one reason she wouldn't be a good wife for St. John is that she's much more plain-looking than he is, Diana replies, "Plain! You? Not at all. You are much too pretty, as well as too good, to be grilled alive in Calcutta." These aren't the words of a sister hoping to help her brother convince a woman to marry him; they're the author's affirmation that Jane is beautiful and should have a greater sense of self-worth. Diana's and Rochester's affection for Jane and their awareness of the passionate, fun-loving woman behind the repressed Lowood graduate provide a subtle commentary on Jane's own narrative that seems to channel Charlotte Brontë's own feelings.

Writing Style

Refined, Educated, Precise, Intricate

You don't have to read very far in *Jane Eyre* to notice that the syntax and style of the sentences are complex; phrases and clauses are elaborately interwoven, but still feel balanced and exact. For example, at the very beginning of the novel Jane tells us that she's glad she can't take a walk with her cousins: "I never liked long walks, especially on chilly afternoons: dreadful to me was the coming home in the raw twilight, with nipped fingers and toes, and a heart saddened by the chidings of Bessie, the nurse, and humbled by the consciousness of my physical inferiority to Eliza, John, and Georgiana Reed" (1.1.2). You could convey the same information by saying, "I never liked long walks. I hate coming home in the dark and having cold fingers and toes, and I hate getting yelled at and feeling pathetic compared to my cousins." But Jane's sentences are refined; we can tell that she's educated, that she never over-simplifies her ideas, and that she likes to give us a series of ideas in an interconnected web, instead of a group of short statements.

What's Up With the Title?

So, this is a novel about a woman named Jane Eyre, and it's titled *Jane Eyre*. Seems pretty obvious, that one. But think about this for a second: the novel itself is *Jane Eyre*, but the main character is Jane Eyre, so we're going to get confused a lot about whether we're talking about the whole book or just the character. This confusion isn't accidental: this novel (like most novels named for the hero or heroine) is all about the ways in which the main character is and isn't the same as the book that bears her name.

And what about that name – "Jane Eyre"? The "Jane" part makes us think "plain Jane" – it's an everyday, basic sort of name, not flowery, not snazzy; it fades into the background, which is something Jane's going to try to do a lot – or at least she'll *claim* that's what she wants to do. And what about her last name, "Eyre"? That's not a name we've heard anywhere else. It's usually pronounced "air," by the way, suggesting airy-fairy sorts of qualities – and Rochester frequently accuses Jane of being like a sprite or a fairy or some other supernatural creature. Maybe it also suggests someone who "gives herself airs," someone snooty, uppity, or haughty, which is how the other servants in Rochester's household, like Mrs. Fairfax, seem to perceive Jane – as someone "with her nose in the air." You also might be tempted to pronounce Jane's last name as "ear," like the thing on the side of your head, and Jane is going to do a lot of listening and eavesdropping and being a sounding board.

But we're getting ahead of ourselves; if you want to know more about Jane, head over to the "Character Clues" section and read about her there. Right now we're thinking about that subtitle, *An Autobiography*. After all, this isn't Charlotte Brontë's autobiography. It's not even Currer Bell's autobiography. (See "Brain Snacks" for more on the pseudonym "Currer Bell.") But the novel *is* Jane's own retelling of her life story to the reader (see "Narrator Point of View"). In fact, Charlotte Brontë uses a lot of her own life experience to make Jane a rounded character – Charlotte, like Jane, taught at an unpleasant girls' boarding school, for example – and the book really toes the line between autobiography and fiction. So, not only is *Jane Eyre* going to make us think about the relationship between the protagonist and the text itself – are we talking about Jane Eyre or *Jane Eyre*? – it's also going to make us think about the relationship between the protagonist and the author.

All that from just the four words of the title! Think what'll happen when we actually analyze all 38 chapters! We don't know about you, but we can't wait.

What's Up With the Ending?

Strangely, *Jane Eyre* doesn't end with Jane Eyre herself. Oh, sure, at the beginning of the last chapter, we get that famous line, "Reader, I married him" (3.12.1), and we're excited that we finally get to have the wedding that Jane was denied at the end of Volume II. But the novel seems to be pretty much over the whole wedding thing by this point; after just a few understated paragraphs where Jane tells us about how Rochester's servants take this news, it's suddenly ten years later, Rochester has gotten his sight back, he and Jane chat all the time, and "perfect concord is the result" (3.12.13). Hooray, a happy ending. But what Jane's *really* concerned with telling us at the end isn't how *her* story ended – it's about what happened to lots of the other characters, especially, for some weird reason, St. John Rivers.

St. John Rivers – remember him? The intensely, not to say obsessively, religious cousin who wants to marry Jane, teach her Hindustani, and take her with him on a missionary trip to India? And she's just about willing to go for the last two ideas, but the first one is *definitely* out of the question? Maybe you should brush up on him in the "Character Clues" section if you've forgotten, because the very end of the novel isn't about Jane or her marriage – it's about how St. John *did* go to India on his mission and has basically worked himself to death there. The last line of the book is Jane quoting from one of St. John's letters, in which he accepts his imminent death with the words "Amen; even so come, Lord Jesus!" (3.12.24). That's a pretty weird ending for a book that has been more about "Morality and Ethics" than about "Religion" most of the time. Why, at the very end, does the novel move away from Jane and the marriage plot and toward a consideration of obsession, illness, and overseas travel to other parts of the British Empire?

Well, let's think about how each of those issues has persisted throughout the novel. First, there's St. John's obsession with missionary work. One of the problems in *Jane Eyre* seems to be how to serve other people in the right way – after all, Jane's a servant for most of the book, and a pretty good one, really. That's why St. John wants her to go with him – because she's hardworking and intelligent. But Jane's pretty good at setting the right boundaries for herself, and she can tell that St. John's ideas about service are too intense, too self-sacrificing, too extreme.

Second, there's illness. St. John's own sickness seems to come from overworking himself and just generally being keyed up about things, but other characters sicken and die without causing their illness themselves, like Helen Burns and Mrs. Reed. And, of course, there are other moments of affliction that don't result in death: Mr. Rochester's blindness, Mason's wound, Jane's fever after she runs away from Rochester. Of course, part of it is just that illnesses were more dangerous in the nineteenth-century because medical science wasn't as advanced, but there's more going on here. Jane is the nurse for most of these characters, but St. John she can't help. She can't even ease his suffering, as she does for Helen or Mrs. Reed, and she certainly can't cure him.

Third and last, there's "overseas," foreign places that are and aren't part of Britain. India, St. John's destination (before Heaven, that is), reminds us of the West Indies, where Bertha came from and where Mr. Rochester made his money. Travel to and from these colonial outposts is definitely a major theme here (see our discussion of "Foreignness and 'The Other'" in the "Themes" section).

So maybe in one way St. John is taking all these loose ends, all these aspects of the novel that are too intense, too dangerous, or too impossible for Jane to sort out – extremes of self-sacrifice in serving others, dangerous incurable fevers, and whatever intangible weirdness Bertha and Rochester bring back with them from the Caribbean – and taking them out to a distant colony so that England can feel "safe." Maybe St. John is the opposite of Bertha, taking away, instead of bringing, a near-insane intensity that degenerates into illness. And maybe the novel ends by thinking about these issues because they're more provocative – maybe even more interesting – than Jane getting married. Even Jane seems more interested in St. John's work than her own marriage, even if she doesn't want to go with him – after all, they're exchanging letters. *Jane Eyre* seems at first to have a traditional marriage plot, but talks itself into following a different plot – one for which St. John, not Jane, is the end point. Do you buy that? We're not sure, but it's a good place to start. Er, end, that is. You get the idea.

Did You Know?

Trivia

- Charlotte Brontë published *Jane Eyre* under the pseudonym "Currer Bell" because there was a lot of prejudice against women writers in the Victorian period. It's not that women weren't writing – there were lots of women writing novels and poems and getting published in the nineteenth century – it's just that critics automatically assumed that their work sucked. Charlotte wanted her work to be read on its merits, so she took a pseudonym that made her gender totally unclear. (It's important that "Currer Bell" is a *gender-neutral* name, NOT a male pseudonym for a female author like "George Eliot.") (Source)
- When Charlotte Brontë was a student in Brussels, she fell passionately in love with her

teacher, Monsieur Heger, who was married and had a family of his own and was *so* not interested in her. *Jane Eyre* is in some ways a wish-fulfillment fantasy for Brontë in which the young woman student/teacher does get to seduce her master. (Source)

- Charlotte Brontë was part of a strange and literary family: her sisters Emily and Anne also published novels and poems, and her brother Branwell was a wild drunk and drug addict who added some serious weirdness to their lives. Charlotte's mother and two other sisters (Maria and Elizabeth) all died when Charlotte was very young. (Source)
- The 1966 novel *Wide Sargasso Sea* retells the back-story of *Jane Eyre* from the perspective of Bertha Mason and explores issues of race, class, and gender.
- In 1979, Sandra Gilbert and Susan Gubar published *The Madwoman in the Attic: The Woman Writer and the Nineteenth-Century Literary Imagination* which almost instantly became one of the most important works of feminist literary criticism. The "madwoman in the attic," of course, is a reference to Bertha Mason. (Source)
- Charlotte Brontë dedicated *Jane Eyre* (starting with the second edition) to William Makepeace Thackeray, the author of *Vanity Fair*. Unfortunately, Thackeray was married to a mentally ill woman and had written his own novel about a social-climbing governess, so the dedication caused a lot of unpleasant gossip. (Source)
- *Jane Eyre* is a traditional Victorian three-volume novel. When the novel was originally published, it came out in three long installments, a little bit like the three volumes of a trilogy (think Tolkien's *Lord of the Rings* books), although there was just one main plot, not three separate ones. Libraries would buy the set of three volumes, and then they could check all three of them out to different people, so more than one person could be reading a different part of the book at the same time. In those days you paid to check books out of the library, so this was a big money-maker for the libraries and the publishers. After all three volumes had come out, the novel was usually reissued in a single-volume edition, which everyone bought so they could have the newest, snazziest version, and the publishers made even more money. (Does this sound familiar? Think about all those boxed sets of *Harry Potter* books. Scholastic is raking it in, man.) (Source)

Steaminess Rating

PG

Jane Eyre is a Victorian novel, and so it does have a somewhat repressed feel. Even though one major strand of the plot is the passionate romance between Jane and Rochester, we don't get too many steamy, bodice-ripping bedroom scenes. There are a few moments where the heat gets turned up, such as the time Jane discovers Rochester literally smoldering in his bed and has to throw cold water on him. OK, that one's actually about extinguishing the flames, but it's still about standing in the dark with the man you love while his clothes are clinging to him, right?

We do get some passionate embraces, declarations of love, sudden kisses, and a few indecent proposals. We learn about Rochester's sleazy past, which involves French, Italian, and

German mistresses – heck, he doesn't even know if Adèle is his daughter or not. Bertha's main charm as a young woman was sex appeal. Rochester tries to commit bigamy or get Jane to live with him as his wife without getting married, and at points Jane seems to be teasing him and arguing with him to keep him from losing control and ravishing her. In fact there's a lot of sex here, even though most of it happens "offstage."

Allusions and Cultural References

Literature and Philosophy

- Thomas Bewick, *A History of British Birds* (I.1, II.6)
- Samuel Richardson, *Pamela* (I.1)
- Oliver Goldsmith, *History of Rome* (I.1)
- Jonathan Swift, *Gulliver's Travels* (I.3, II.6)
- John Milton, *Paradise Lost* (I.13, II.2, III.8)
- William Shakespeare, *Hamlet* (I.15, II.9)
- William Shakespeare, *King Lear* (II.4)
- William Shakespeare, *Much Ado About Nothing* (II.5)
- *The Arabian Nights* (II.6)
- Friedrich Schiller, *The Robbers* (III.3, III.8)
- Sir Walter Scott, *The Lay of the Last Minstrel* (III.5, III.8)
- Samuel Taylor Coleridge, *The Rime of the Ancient Mariner* (III.6)
- Sir Walter Scott, *Marmion* (III.6, III.7)

Mythological References

- Bluebeard's castle (I.11)
- the Gytrash (I.12)
- the Sphinx (I.14)
- the *ignis fatuus* ("false fire") (II.1, II.7, III.2)
- Diana (II.2)
- the Sybil (II.3)
- Hercules (II.9)
- Danae (II.9)
- vampires (II.10)
- the upas-tree (III.1)
- Apollo (III.11)
- Vulcan (III.11)

Biblical References

There are a LOT of Biblical references in Jane Eyre; here are some of the most important.

General:

- Psalms (I.4, II.4, II.11)
- the New Testament (I.6)
- Matthew (I.7, II.11, III.1)
- Proverbs 15:17 15:17 (I.8)
- Job (I.15)
- Luke (III.9)

Specific Stories and People:

- Rebecca and Isaac at the well of Nahor (II.3)
- Samson (II.9, III.1, III.11)
- King Ahasuerus (II.9)
- Lot's wife (III.5)
- Nebuchadnezzar in the fields (III.11)
- Saul and David (III.11)

Specific Verses:

- 1 Kings 19:11-12 (II.4)
- 2 Samuel 12:3 (III.1)
- Zechariah 4:10 (III.3)
- Philippians 4:7 (III.4)
- 1 Corinthians 15:53 (III.6)
- 1 Timothy 5:8 (III.8)
- Amos 4:11 (III.9)
- Zechariah 3:2 (III.9)
- John 9:4 (III.9)
- Isaiah 34:4 (III.9)
- Song of Songs 2:11 (III.11)
- Psalms 23:4 (III.11)
- Luke 2:19 (III.11)
- Genesis 2:23 (III.12)
- Revelation 14:5 (III.12)
- 1 Corinthians 9:25 (III.12)
- Matthew 25:21 (III.12)
- Revelation 22:20 (III.12)

Best of the Web

Movie or TV Productions

Jane Eyre – 2006 BBC Mini-Series
http://www.imdb.com/title/tt0780362/
Starring Ruth Wilson and Toby Stephens, this TV adaptation is up-to-date, well-paced, and has high production values. Definitely our favorite adaptation so far, and pretty good as a study aid, too.

Jane Eyre – 1996 Film
http://www.imdb.com/title/tt0116684/
This is the most recent big-budget film version of *Jane Eyre*, directed by the famous and fantastic Franco Zeffirelli.

Jane Eyre – 1944 Film
http://www.imdb.com/title/tt0036969/
This is the "vintage classic" film version, starring Orson Welles and Joan Fontaine. Not as snazzy and new as some of the other versions, but charming in its own way, if you like that sort of thing.

I Walked With a Zombie – 1943 Film
http://www.imdb.com/title/tt0036027/
This classic horror flick is very, very loosely based on *Jane Eyre* and set in the West Indies. Weird and wacky, it really explores the theme of "Foreignness and 'The Other'" in an interesting way.

Videos

"Money Matters & Flirting"
http://youtube.com/watch?v=bSrpvMSuhPM
In this scene from the 2006 BBC miniseries adaptation of *Jane Eyre*, Jane asks to visit her dying aunt and she and Rochester argue over how much he'll pay her at this point for the work she's done so far. This is a really useful video because it can be difficult to understand how flirtatious and playful this scene is in the book.

"*Jane Eyre*: Happily Ever After"
http://youtube.com/watch?v=CIflJKtVb08
A scene from the 2006 BBC miniseries adaptation of *Jane Eyre* that does exactly what it says in the title! This ending is a bit more sexed up than we think makes sense for the Victorian period, but hey, whatever.

Audios

Free *Jane Eyre* Audiobook
http://librivox.org/jane-eyre-by-charlotte-bront/
Complete, unabridged reading of all 38 chapters, available for free online from LibriVox!

Vintage *Jane Eyre* Radio Adaptation
http://nostalgic-radio.com/2007/10/12/jane-eyre-by-charlotte-bronte.aspx
CBS Radio Mystery Theater version of the story, recorded in 1977. CAUTION: this is a very loose adaptation, so it's a lot of fun but might not help you learn all the details of the plot of the novel.

Images

The Governess
http://www.victorianweb.org/painting/redgrave/paintings/2.jpg
An 1844 oil painting of a Victorian governess by Richard Redgrave.

Jane Eyre 1944 Movie Poster
http://upload.wikimedia.org/wikipedia/en/3/3a/Jane_Eyre.jpeg
Poster from the classic 1944 film adaptation starring Orson Welles and Joan Fontaine.

Documents

Full Text of *Jane Eyre*
http://www.gutenberg.org/etext/1260
The entire novel online, complete and unabridged, from Project Gutenberg. Read it on screen or download it to your computer.

Oxford World's Classics Edition of *Jane Eyre* on Google Books
http://books.google.com/books?vid=ISBN0192839659&id=nELi3-TkzqcC&printsec=frontcover&dq=Jane+Eyre#PPR9,M1
This is only a preview – you may not be able to read the whole text of the novel here without paying, and we don't recommend paying, because you can read the novel at Project Gutenberg for free. BUT, we do recommend that you check this out, because you *will* be able to read the introduction to the novel by Sally Shuttleworth, which is really useful.

Penguin Classics Edition of *Jane Eyre* on Google Books
http://books.google.com/books?vid=ISBN0142437204&id=z5ZLjalQNbAC&printsec=frontcover&dq=Jane+Eyre
Again, this is only a preview, but you can read the introduction by Michael Mason.

"Reader, I Shagged Him" by Tanya Gold
http://books.guardian.co.uk/departments/classics/story/0,,1445404,00.html
An article from the British newspaper *The Guardian* which explains Charlotte Brontë's dark imagination and how her biographer, Elizabeth Gaskell, made her seem more prim and proper. Gold rejects the idea that *Jane Eyre* is repressed and gets deep into its sexual undertones.

"Jane Eyre Runs for President" by Sean Carman
http://www.mcsweeneys.net/2008/1/3carman.html
A parody article in which Jane Eyre is one of the candidates during the 2008 presidential election. (Can you guess who she represents?)

The Life of Charlotte Brontë by Elizabeth Gaskell

http://lang.nagoya-u.ac.jp/~matsuoka/EG-Charlotte-1.html
Full text of Gaskell's famous 1857 biography of Brontë. This work is interesting because Gaskell was a contemporary of Brontë's, but it is somewhat whitewashed – make sure you read more recent biographies, too.

Websites

Charlotte Brontë: An Overview
http://www.victorianweb.org/authors/bronte/cbronte/eyreov.html
Commentary and background on *Jane Eyre* from a variety of eminent scholars. Part of "The Victorian Web," a large scholarly project devoted to creating online archives of academic material related to nineteenth-century British literature and culture.

Jane Eyre Background Info
http://academic.brooklyn.cuny.edu/english/melani/cs6/bronte.html
This is a website created by Lilia Melani, an Associate Professor of English at Brooklyn College. It's short and to the point, and it has some good information about context.

2221706R00072

Printed in Great Britain
by Amazon.co.uk, Ltd.,
Marston Gate.